PURSUE DAILY
The Simple Pursuit of Knowing God, His Word, and Yourself.

EMILY N. GREEN

PURSUE DAILY

All Scripture quotations, unless otherwise indicated, are taken from the Holy Bible, New International Version NIV©.

Bold in Scripture quotations reflect the author's added emphasis.

Paperback ISBN 979-8-218-35094-9

Copyright © 2023 by Emily N. Green

All rights reserved. No part of this book may be reproduced or used in any manner without written permission of the copyright owner except for the use of quotations.

First Paperback Edition 2023

Published by Emily N. Green.

www.emilyngreen.com

DEDICATION

To Austin, my husband, and Bill Norris, my Papaw.

Austin, you, other than the Lord, are the most important thing to me. You are constant, brave, and kind. You always have the right words to say and never fail to keep Scripture at the center of our conversations. You lead and protect our family with boldness, and your love for God, people, and His creation inspires me daily. I dedicate this book to you.

Papaw, I remember going to your book signing party as a kid and seeing the boxes and boxes of books in your office with your name on them. I had always known I loved to write, but seeing you become a published author lit the fire in me to do the same. It is the privilege of my life to follow in your footsteps. I wish the world were as fortunate as I have been to hear the stories of your bravery, service, and sacrifice. At 91 years old, I know you have left a legacy that will forever outlive you and impact the generations to come. In addition to your two books, this book will be yet another testament to the miracle, testimony, and inspiration that is your life. I dedicate this book to you.

CONTENTS

	Introduction	1
1	Pursue God	5
2	Pursue Faith	19
3	Pursue Righteousness	29
4	Pursue Love	39
5	Pursue Peace	51
6	Pursue Purity	63
7	Pursue Humility	79
8	Pursue Forgiveness	93
9	Pursue Awareness	105
10	Pursue Your Gifting	121
11	Pursue Health	133
12	Pursue Community	149
13	Pursue the End Goal	161
	Conclusion	173
	Discussion Questions	175
	Notes	179

ACKNOWLEDGMENTS

Thank you to my editors, Dr. Christopher Hanna, Angela Norris, and Douglas Norris, and my cover designer, Emily Reasner. A special thank you to all my friends and family who have prayed for me and this project over the years. May the Lord do with it what He wills.

INTRODUCTION

"Therefore, if anyone cleanses himself from what is dishonorable, he will be a vessel for honorable use, set apart as holy, useful to the master of the house, ready for every good work."
2 Timothy 2:21 NIV

Welcome to *Pursue Daily*. I am so happy you're reading this book! This journey you're about to begin is filled with so much hope, fun, and growth. Before we get started, I want to take some time to prepare you for our time together. We're about to become *really* close friends and grow a lot together. So, before we set out on this journey, let's talk about what exactly *Pursue Daily* is and how you can get the most out of your experience.

This book is called *Pursue Daily* because it is designed to help you go on a daily journey. When you became a Christian, you were saved, which means you will have eternal life with God in heaven. However, there's a lot for us to do here on earth before we step into eternity with Him. This book is designed to help you make the most of that time. I will do my best to share biblical truths, insights, and scholarly knowledge with you—but don't worry. I built this whole thing to be simple, easy to understand, and highly impactful.

Maybe you've heard this quote: "It's not about the destination; it's about the journey." I'm here to tell you that is so true! *Pursue Daily* was created to help you enjoy the journey of Christianity and was designed with three things in mind:

1. We're in the process of sanctification.
2. Consistency creates habits, and healthy habits lead to maturity.
3. There's always more.

We're in the process of sanctification.

Sanctification is the action or process of being freed from sin or purified.[1] Theologian Gregg Allison also says that "sanctification—specifically progressive sanctification—is the cooperative work of God and Christians by which ongoing transformation into greater Christlikeness occurs."[2] The keywords in these definitions are "process" and "progressive." As we just mentioned, being forgiven from our sins happens when we accept Jesus into our lives. However, there is a *process* that we must endure and progress through to become completely free and clean from our past.

As we discuss each topic in this book, please understand that none of these characteristics or goals are achieved overnight. Each topic is something that we must (you guessed it) *pursue daily*. It's okay if it doesn't click right away. Everyone's process of sanctification looks different; what matters most is that you're committed to the process!

Consistency creates habits, and healthy habits lead to maturity.

Is anyone else out there a creature of habit? I sure am! While sometimes it can be a bad thing, it's a fantastic thing many times. Being a creature of habit means being a creature of consistency, and consistency often leads to maturity.

As you read through the upcoming pages, I encourage you to remember that consistency creates habits. When we commit to the process of sanctification and choose to work on our character and faith consistently, we'll automatically create healthy habits in our lives. When we build healthy habits, we are well on our way to spiritual maturity.

Spiritual maturity can be defined as many things, but I think of it as a quality that a Christian can grow into based on experience, knowledge, and commitment. Spiritual maturity is not measured by length of time; instead, it's measured by one's quality of relationship with the Lord. When we reach the position of quality faith, we have reached a level of spiritual maturity that is inspiring, helpful, and worthy of sharing with others.

There's always more.

Regardless of how long you've been walking with the Lord, remember that there is always more. Maybe you've had a relationship with God for years. Maybe you just started a relationship with God recently. You may even be reading this book and have no clue who God is, and if that's the case, please keep reading!

There is always more with God, and I believe He has something He wants to teach us in the upcoming pages. So, let's approach this journey together with humility, grace, and open hearts—you never know what divine appointment God has made to meet with you!

PURSUE DAILY

Alright, friends! We're close to getting started, and I can hardly wait! Thank you for going on this journey, and thank you for committing to pursue daily. The last thing I'll ask of you is this: Don't make this journey alone! Invite a friend, family member, or small group to walk out this journey of pursuing God daily with you. Trust me—it'll be worth it!

Now, let's begin!

1

PURSUE GOD

"Come near to God, and He will come near to you."
James 4:8 NIV

WHAT GOES DOWN MUST COME UP

Have you ever been in a situation where you weren't prepared for what was happening?

My husband, Austin, and I know a bit about that.

One of our first dates was hiking an hour or so north of where he grew up in Alabama. We had heard about this beautiful trail that led to a waterfall, and while I'm not the adventurous type, I enjoy a good view, so I was down to try it out. The weekend before this, we had gone on another hike. That hike was in a park and was paved, shaded, and safe. There was a nice parking lot for our cars and a welcome center with maps of the property. Before this hike,

I hadn't been on a hike in years, and I was pleasantly surprised at the calm and comforting experience it was. Therefore, I was expecting this experience to be a lot like that one.

We were sitting at the breakfast table that Saturday morning, and Austin suggested we try a hike at this new park. I agreed. However, I only had my "nicer" tennis shoes, shirt, and leggings (ladies, you all understand the difference between your *actual workout outfit* and your *nice workout outfit*). Even so, I figured I would be okay with my "nicer" workout outfit since the hike would be easy.

We had only eaten bananas for breakfast, but I thought we'd be okay since this hike would be paved, shaded, and safe, just like the trail we had done the weekend before. We changed, packed up, and began our drive. After driving through some twisty roads in the Alabama countryside, Austin pulled the car over to the side of the road. There was a gravel lot and a few other cars.

I was confused.

"Babe?" I said. "Are you okay? Why are we stopping?"

Austin looked at me with a twinkle in his eye and grinned. "We're here."

I would like to point out that "here" was *not* what I thought it would be. Instead of a nice parking lot and welcome center, there was a simple gravel lot. There were no bathrooms and no pavement—just rocks and dirt. The path started *down* the hill, which meant, at some point, we'd have to come back *up*—most likely when we were tired and hot and dirty.

All at once, my mood went from "This is the best thing ever!" to "Can we please leave?" I knew Austin wanted to try it out, however, so I kept a smile on my face.

We began our trek down the hillside, walking in a single-file line, hugging the edge of the hill to avoid the drop-off on the other side of the path. Roots, rocks, and creatures were everywhere. All we had in our bellies were bananas, and all we had in our hands were little eight-ounce water bottles—not even a whole water bottle!

Even so, we kept going.

About an hour and a half into our journey, we saw people coming back up the trail, sweaty, hot, and wet. We could hear the waterfall in the distance and got excited. They must've just been there! We sat on a rock with our fellow hikers and asked how far away we were from the attraction. We knew we must be close!

With eager hearts, we awaited their answer. To my dismay, when we asked, "Are we close to the bottom?" a lady gave a little laugh and said, "Ha, you're halfway there."

Halfway.

Another hour and a half to go.

At this point, we were exhausted. The eight ounces of water we had lasted about 13 seconds. We had no food. We were approaching the middle of the day, which, in Alabama, means HOT.

But the waterfall...We could *hear* it. We were so close. It would take an hour and a half more to get there and three hours uphill to return to our car. Was it worth it?

After contemplating our next move, Austin stood up and said, "Okay, babe, let's go." I let out a sigh of relief. I was ecstatic that he was ready to return to the car. I had zero faith that we would make the entire hike if we went to the waterfall! At his cue, I jumped off the rock, and we started walking—in opposite directions.

He headed toward the waterfall. I headed toward the car. When we realized we were going in separate directions, we stopped and looked at each other. We gave each other the same look, the look that says, *"You've got to be kidding me."*

We stood there for a moment, and then, *naturally*, I began to explain my concerns.

"We don't have enough water."

"We didn't eat enough for this."

"We (I) don't have the right clothing."

"We didn't know it would take six hours."

"We weren't prepared for this."

After listening to me defend my case for why we would be insane to continue this trek, my amazing husband didn't fight me *too* hard on the decision to go back to the car. With heavy (and frustrated) hearts, we started our journey back up the mountain without a visit to the waterfall. No Instagram-worthy pictures. No feeling of "success." Just defeat, disappointment, and a lot of hunger and dehydration.

Just like Austin and I were taking a journey to the waterfall that day, all of us are taking a journey together to pursue the fullness of who God is. However, if we're not adequately prepared for what's ahead, we won't be able to succeed. Austin and I didn't have the right fuel or tools to complete our hike. In the same way, when it comes to taking a spiritual journey, a lot of us are missing the right fuel and tools to be successful. To build an effective spiritual journey and pursue a godly lifestyle daily, we must start by pursuing God Himself.

Pursuing God is not about following all the rules, going to church every time the doors are open, not having fun, and not enjoying life. Pursuing God is about building a relationship with Him, enjoying who He is, and experiencing the life He always wanted for us. Sure, we'll talk about church and serving and making good choices later, but to best be prepared for this journey, you have to know that **God is more interested in who you are rather than what you do.** He'd rather know your heart than your track record. He cares about who you are over what you can achieve for Him.

I would also present to you that He wants the same thing from you. Pursuing God doesn't mean trying to get something *from* Him—wealth, fame, popularity, etc. We pursue God because we want to know more *of* Him. We want to build a relationship with Him, not just be a part of a religion. Therefore, I pray that you take on these pages with fresh eyes and an open heart, truly believing that God has more in store for you. It all begins with you discovering more of Him!

WHAT DOES IT MEAN TO PURSUE GOD?
"Come near to God, and He will come near to you."
James 4:8 NIV

To "pursue God" means to draw near to Him, as our theme verse for this chapter, James 4:8, tells us. The phrase "draw near" in this verse means to "approach" or "join one thing to another."[1] This phrase means that when we pursue God, we step toward becoming further united with Him. As we draw near to God, we are building our relationship with Him, not just following the rules of religion.

When building a relationship with someone, step one is to learn more about them. Have you ever been to a summer camp or vacation with people you didn't know very well at first, and then after sharing a bunkbed with them for a week, you were automatic besties? It's because you got to know them by spending time together! You shared common activities, common space, and most likely some common interests. You asked them questions, engaged in conversation, spent time with them, and found out more about them. Before you knew it, you had built a relationship with them.

Building a relationship with God is a lot like building a relationship with a person. Pursuing God means taking a step toward Him every day—to ask a question, engage in conversation, spend time with Him, and ultimately build a relationship. According to the book of Joshua, God's presence is with us wherever we go,[2] which means that every activity, place, and interest we invest in is not done alone. Whether you realize it or not, you and God actually share a lot of the same things! Knowing God is present in every moment—soccer practice, worship rehearsal, taking a test, sending an email—allows us to build our relationship with Him by acknowledging His companionship.

WHY SHOULD I PURSUE GOD?
"We love because He first loved us."
1 John 4:19 NIV

Throughout the Bible, marriage symbolizes God's relationship with the Church (aka us). According to Genesis 2:24, when you marry someone, you are "united" to them, and the two of you "become one flesh." What makes marriage so powerful is the uniting of two individuals, man and woman, to become one powerhouse unit. The same is true in a relationship with God. Just as we become one with our spouse when we get married, we become joined with God when we get saved.

However, if that was it, would there *really* be a relationship? If Austin and I got married and never spoke to each other again, would we really be a part of each other's lives? Probably not. Even though we're in a relationship with each other, we still have to *pursue* each other every day, and it's the same in our relationship with God! We must pursue God daily because we're building a relationship with Him. Daily time with Him is essential because our relationship with God is the foundation for everything else. Pursuing God daily creates a firm foundation for your relationship with the Lord.

Without a real relationship with God, your foundation will be cracked. Just as a house cannot stand on a cracked foundation, our spiritual lives cannot survive on a foundation that isn't sufficient. When it comes to Christianity, your foundation needs regular attention—like, *everyday attention.*

Do you know you have an enemy working overtime to crack your foundation? If the devil can break the foundation, the entire house will fall. Take the Scripture, for example, that says, "Strike the shepherd, and the sheep of the flock will be scattered."[3] Do you think the enemy is going after every "sheep"? Do you think he's going after every little thing you do? Do you really think he's wasting all his time and dividing his efforts to attack your sports team, work-life, eating habits, sleeping patterns, relationships, emotions, and everything else you've got going on? Why would he divide his efforts when he knows that if he can get you disconnected from pursuing God, everything else will crumble?

The enemy is spending all his time attacking your spiritual foundation because if he can disrupt that, he can destroy everything else. Whether or not you believe it, you are a triune being comprised of a spirit, soul, and body.[4] You are a triune being because you are made in God's image,[5] and God Himself is a triune being.[6] Out of the three parts, your spirit is the most important.

My pastor always says, "We aren't human beings having a spiritual experience; we are spiritual beings having a human experience."[7] What does this mean for you? Well, this means that your life is not built on physical things; your life is built on a spiritual foundation, and without creating a firm spiritual foundation by pursuing God, your life cannot be what God always intended for it to be.

As we take this journey to pursue God daily together, remember: **God took the first step.**[8] This relationship isn't something you're trying to build with fear of rejection or heartache; this is a relationship that you can invest in, knowing that you will never be let down. Every minute, every action, and every word used to pursue God and build your spiritual foundation is not wasted, unseen, or unheard. Don't let the enemy wreak havoc in your life; pursue God daily and find comfort in His shelter.

As the theme verse says for this section, "We love because [God] first loved us."[9] We love God and pursue Him out of His love for us, not for what He can do or what it will mean for us. Take the pressure off, friend. You can't earn God's love. You can't earn His protection. You can't earn His salvation. It's a gift that's freely given,[10] so enjoy the advantage of knowing God by pursuing more of Him every day and building a solid spiritual foundation.

HOW DO I PURSUE GOD?

"Enter His gates with thanksgiving and His courts with praise; give thanks to Him and praise His name."
Psalm 100:4 NIV

Now that we've clarified what pursuing God means and why it's important, let's get practical. Following are action steps you can start today to begin pursuing God, and you may just be surprised at the simplicity of each step.

There are three foundational ways to pursue God: **worshiping, praying, and reading the Bible**. If you've been around church for any period, you've heard about these three things. These actions have also been coined as a part of the "spiritual disciplines" of Christianity,[11] notably some of the most needed disciplines to grow your relationship with God.

When practiced out of a desire to know God more, these spiritual disciplines will help you pursue God daily and build a solid spiritual foundation that the enemy can't even get close to cracking.

Worship

"Therefore, I urge you, brothers and sisters, in view of God's mercy, to offer your bodies as a living sacrifice, holy and pleasing to God—this is your true and proper worship." - Romans 12:1 NIV

In Romans 12:1, Paul encourages the Romans to "offer [their] bodies as a living sacrifice, holy and pleasing to God," adding that "this is [the] true and proper worship." Worship is more than songs, music, and lyrics; it's a lifestyle, something we can inhabit every moment of every day.

When we worship, we're not just singing a note or playing a chord. When we worship, we give ourselves to be used by God. When we lay down what we want for what He wants, or when we take time to acknowledge Him and His presence, we're worshiping.

Here's the main thing to know about worship: When we worship, we're taking the focus off ourselves and putting it on God. We're saying, "God, you are the one I want to pursue more than anything. You're the most important thing in my life." Psalm 100:4 is my absolute favorite verse about worship because, within these words, the Psalmist has listed out for us how to worship God in this way:

"Enter into His gates with thanksgiving, and into His courts with praise: be thankful unto Him, and bless His name." - Psalm 100:4 NIV

We enter God's presence through thanksgiving and praise, and thanking and praising God can look different for all of us. Here are a few ways we can worship, according to the Bible:

- Telling God thank you (Psalm 100:4)

- Praising Him (Psalm 100:4)
- Speaking His Name (Psalm 100:4)
- Singing (Psalm 149:1)
- Dancing (Psalm 149:3)
- Shouting (Psalm 98:4)
- Creating music with instruments (Psalm 149:3)
- Surrendering our lives to God (Romans 12:1)
- Giving (2 Corinthians 9:6-15)

Regardless of what worship looks like for you, it's not only a way to pursue God but also a way to wage war on the enemy. Worship and thankfulness are the greatest weapons you have; when you don't know what else to do, start here. Turn on a song. Raise your hands. Talk to God. Shout. Dance. Serve. Thank Him. Surrender your life to Him. You'll be surprised at how close you feel to God and how far away you feel from your troubles.

Prayer

"Look to the Lord and His strength; seek His face always." - 1 Chronicles 16:11 NIV

On top of worship, we also have the incredible tool of prayer. In short, prayer is communication with God. Communication is a process that focuses on the interaction between a sender and a receiver.[12] Therefore, to effectively communicate with God, there must be an interaction on both parts. Prayer is making your requests known to God and pursuing Him with your time and words, but it is also listening to Him and what He has to say.

We know that prayer is important because we see great men and women of the faith throughout the Bible pray. Adam and Eve walked and talked with God.[13] Abraham discussed the possibility of a child with God.[14] Moses asked for guidance and to see God's glory.[15] David asked God for protection.[16] Daniel spoke to God three times a day publicly.[17] Jesus asked God to take His death sentence away from Him, but He also asked for His will to be done.[18]

All these great characters and many more spoke to God regularly, and it never looked the same. Adam and Eve took a walk with God. Abraham and God discussed under the open sky. Daniel spoke to God on his balcony with the windows wide open. Jesus went to be by Himself and talked to God in the middle of the night.

While the circumstances and look of prayers can vary, they are powerful because they are a conversation with God. Like any good conversation, it consists of both talking and listening. God desires for us to tell Him what's on our hearts, but we must remember that He already knows. We can spend time verbalizing every little detail to Him, but we should also invest in our time with God by listening to Him.

The more we listen, the more we know, and the more we know, the more there is to pursue. It's nothing too crazy or flashy or loud or theatrical—just listening to God and talking to Him.

God's Word
"For the word of God is alive and active. Sharper than any double-edged sword, it penetrates even to dividing soul and spirit, joints and marrow; it judges the thoughts and attitudes of the heart." - Hebrews 4:12 NIV

The Bible is God's Holy Word. It's what He left behind for us to live by, follow, study, and enjoy. The Bible isn't just some old history book or collection of rules; this Book is the most important thing you will ever read.

The Bible isn't just a book that can be found in a hotel room drawer or on your bedside table; the Bible is a weapon! It's a lamp to our feet and a light to our path.[19] It's a guide to all we do! The

Bible is Holy Spirit inspired,[20] meaning that all words written in this Book are words God Himself wanted us to have from Him. The value of the written word is that it never fades away.

As believers in Jesus, we must protect the Word of God at all costs. The Bible is infallible (incapable of being wrong) and inerrant (without error or fault). These words mean that everything you read in the Scripture—whether you agree with it or not—is true, correct, and pure. There is no fault in the Word of God. Sure, some arguments say verses have been "misinterpreted" by translators, but let's be honest. It's the Bible, God's Holy Word. Do you *really* think that God would allow His Word to be twisted so much from His original intent? Do you *really* believe God isn't powerful enough to preserve His commands and heart in His own book? To pick and choose from Scripture and justify some verses but not others is a form of pride. It's an act that displays to God that we know how best to run our lives, and we'll only agree with His Word when it agrees with us. I don't know about you, but I don't want my God to agree with me all the time; if He did, it wouldn't make Him God.

The way we know God's Word is to read it. I hear from people all the time that they desire to know God's voice so they can discern what He wants them to do. I would agree that we probably all desire that at some point!

If you desire to know God's voice, you've got to know God's Word because here's the truth: God will rarely say something to you that He hasn't already said in His Word. Moreover, God will never say something to you that *contradicts* what is in His Word. God is consistent. He's the same yesterday, today, and forever.[21] What He speaks to you today will align with what's already in His Word.

Do you want to know how to make decisions? Do you want to know how to be a better friend, child, spouse, employee, boss, or human? Do you want to know how to live with purpose? Do you want to protect the Word of God? Get into His Word!

You can find everything you're looking for within the pages of Genesis to Revelation. As you learn more about God by pursuing Him through His Word, you will have more knowledge and understanding to protect His Word and values in our world today. Don't know where to begin? Pick a spot, and dive in! Start with the Gospel of John, get to know the character of Jesus, and then keep reading. I promise that the God you come to know in the pages of your Bible will be alive, vibrant, and active!

As you learn and experience more, these disciplines will grow with you. However, I encourage you to keep these foundational assets from becoming simple items on a checklist. These disciplines aren't steppingstones that, once mastered, move you on to "better" things like serving in the church or even leading in ministry. I hope you experience the joy of serving and leading, but please know that you never outgrow worship. You never outgrow prayer. You never outgrow God's Word. You never outgrow needing a moment with God every single day because you will never outgrow God Himself.

Daily Declaration

"I believe my God is the only God worthy of my worship. I believe that God hears me when I pray and that He wants to talk to me. I believe the Bible is perfect, and I vow to protect its value and holiness no matter what. As I pursue God, I believe I will learn more about Him because there is always more to learn. Ultimately, I believe God is the one true God, and I give Him control of my life."

2

PURSUE FAITH

"So flee youthful passions and pursue righteousness, faith, love, and peace, along with those who call on the Lord from a pure heart."
2 Timothy 2:22 ESV

TRUST FALL

It was going to be my first mission trip and the longest and farthest I had been from my family ever. Sure, we would be staying in the States, but California was a LONG way away from Alabama. We were leaving in a few weeks, and our last task before departing was our missions' training event. This event happened for multiple teams in the woods near our main church campus and lasted all day. Missions' training consisted of obstacle courses, evangelism training, and—you guessed it—team-building exercises.

As our team made our way through the obstacle course, we felt pretty good about ourselves. We had conquered "the wall," where we each had to scale a 10-ft structure, and "the tightrope," where we had to make it through a course without touching the ground. We had even made it through the "lava field," where each person had to walk across a patch of grass without stepping on any obstacles, solely guided by a teammate's voice. It was all fun and games until we arrived at the trust fall.

This trust fall wasn't your average "I fall back, and you catch me" kind of deal. This trust fall consisted of a platform five feet in the air, and each team member had to climb up to it, cross their arms, and fall back, trusting that their teammates would catch them.

I think now would be a good time to tell you two crucial details of this story:

1. I am terrified of heights. You may be saying, "Emily, it was just five feet!" But being five feet off the ground and then adding that my head is also about five feet off the ground makes it feel like ten feet! That's an entire story of a building!
2. My entire mission trip team was *high school girls*.

I get it—girl power, right? I'm not trying to put a stereotype out there, but I'll be honest: my team was not made up of powerhouse women. Spiritually? Absolutely. Physically? That's another story. We all chose to go to Los Angeles for our mission trip. *Los Angeles. California.* Hollywood. Saint Monica Pier. Chipotle. Outlet Malls. *Really* struggling for the Lord.

Anyways, one by one, each girl went up on the platform, and one by one, they all fell back, and we caught them. You could only have a certain number of team members catching at a time, so we switched out now and then. When it was my turn to catch, I strategically placed myself at the end of the line, where I would only catch the feet. I know—I wasn't *actually* helping, but I was doing the team a favor. I knew my strengths, and being trusted to catch someone's head was not one of them.

We caught every girl, no problem. My trust was starting to be built in this team! I was so impressed by how every girl knew her strengths and weaknesses and positioned herself perfectly to contribute.

But then came my turn to fall. And while I had spent the better part of that exercise this far encouraging myself and building trust in my team, it all went away when it came time to get on that platform.

I climbed up there with shaking hands and feet. I would cross my arms and then uncross them. I would look forward and then peek over my shoulder to make sure they would catch me.

"They're too far away from the platform," I thought.

"I'm pretty short. They're in the position to catch someone who's 6' 7". I'm only 5' 3"." "Where's Samantha? She's the strongest out of the group. Why is she standing so close to the platform? She's going to catch my feet! I need her to catch my head!"

I continued to stand there (and yes, I continued to shake). Finally, the leader taking us through the course approached me and said, "Emily, you have to trust your team. You have to fall."

And my response, honest as can be, was, "I don't want to trust my team, and I don't want to fall."

But I knew that I'd have to do it. It was the only way to complete the exercise and get cleared for our trip.

So, fighting every fear rushing through my veins, I took a deep breath, crossed my arms over my chest, and fell.

0.2 seconds later, I was caught by my teammates. It was nothing. I didn't even get a rush of adrenaline. I had spent a total of 10 minutes waiting in fear of falling when it took my team less than a second to catch me.

Sometimes, pursuing faith in God is like doing a trust fall. Faith is believing in God and trusting Him no matter what, even when we're afraid, confused, or lonely. But here's the cool part, friends: What we can spend hours, days, months, even years worrying about, God can take care of in less than a second—and it all starts with faith in Him.

WHAT IS FAITH?

"Now faith is confidence in what we hope for and assurance about what we do not see." Hebrews 11:1 NIV

Oxford Languages defines faith as a "complete trust or confidence in someone or something" or "a strong belief in God or the doctrines of religions, based on spiritual apprehension rather than proof."[1]

Remember what we said in chapter one about religion versus relationship? While we can have faith in doctrine, rules, and religion, we want to live the kind of life where our faith is in God Himself. We don't trust in rules; we trust in the One who made them.

Part of faith is believing in God without having proof. This is an area that can trip a lot of people up. We desire to know and understand everything there is to know about God, but if we knew and understood everything, we wouldn't need Him. We wouldn't need faith.

The original Greek word for faith in New Testament Scripture is *pistis*.[2] This word means a "conviction that God exists and is the creator and ruler of all things, the provider and bestower of eternal salvation through Christ."³ Faith is all about conviction—a belief inside you that, no matter what happens, will never change. Faith in God means that:

1. You believe He exists.
2. You believe He created everything.
3. You believe He is in control of everything.
4. You believe He is the ultimate Provider.
5. You believe He gives eternal salvation.
6. You believe eternal salvation can only come through Jesus Christ.

If you read all those points and agreed, congratulations! You have faith. You have a conviction that God is real, and He is who He says He is. However, even though we have faith, it doesn't mean we've put it into action. We still must pursue it every day because, if we're not careful, our faith can become complacent and dormant, and when it comes time for it to be mobilized, we won't be prepared.

WHY SHOULD I PURSUE FAITH?

"Now faith is confidence in what we hope for and assurance about what we do not see. This is what the ancients were commended for."
Hebrews 11:1-2 NIV

Just like I prepared for the trust fall but then crumbled in the moment, we can have faith and believe in God but falter when a problem arises. We must pursue faith daily to ensure that when the battles come, we're ready for them. Faith is what separates the spectators from the participants. Faith is the vehicle that gets you in the game.

Hebrews 11:1-2 says, "Faith is the confidence in what we hope for and the assurance about what we do not see. This is what the ancients were commended for." If you keep reading Hebrews 11, you'll see a long list of people driven by faith; it's what people praised them for. When we keep reading Hebrews 11 and see a list of people like Abel, Noah, Abraham, Sarah, Isaac, Joseph, and Moses (and that's just the first half of the list!), we know that they're included not for what amazing things they did but because of their *faith*.

Each verse in Hebrews 11:3-31, at least in the New International Version, begins with the phrase "By faith." This phrase is significant to note in our journey to pursuing faith. Regardless of their mission, decisions, or story in the Bible, every person was added to this list because they showed exemplary faith, and everything they accomplished for the Lord could not have been achieved without it.

So, you're asking, "Why should we pursue faith daily?" Well, I will ask you these questions:

Do you want to do something great for God? Do you want to see sick people healed and dead people brought back to life? Do you want to see the lost get saved and spend eternity in heaven with God our Father? Do you want to make an impact on the world? Do you want to use your influence to advance the Kingdom of God? If you answered yes to any of these questions, that's great, but you can't accomplish it without *faith*.

We pursue faith daily because faith is the prerequisite for doing anything significant for God. You don't have to have specific qualifications, a degree, or certain life experiences. Sometimes, God will use those, but God qualifies those He calls, regardless of one's past, present, or future. Irrespective of what you've got in your talents and gifts tool belt, you still need faith. You must believe that God is who He says He is.[4] You must know that He will never leave nor forsake you.[5] You must have a conviction that beyond the shadow of a doubt, God loves you.[6] Why? Because when you step out to achieve something for God, the enemy will step in the way. Every. Single. Time. Isn't that encouraging?

On a serious note, when you decide to write that book, lead that trip, host that group, or sit by that girl who's all alone, there's will be some pushback from the enemy. No one ever said that a Christian life would be easy. In fact, the opposite is true. Even Jesus said to expect trouble![7] If we know that God has called us to do something great, but we also know that there's an enemy who will try to stop us, what do we do? We rely on faith. We rely on God's Word. We rely on our relationship with Him. We rely on His Name.

And while you may not realize it, every time you pursue God, you also pursue faith. Hebrews 11:1 states, "Faith is the assurance of things hoped for." When we have faith, we can rest assured that God will get us through! Every time you pursue faith, you're storing up conviction, belief, and assurance that, when faced with adversity, will push you to keep pursuing all God has in store for you.

HOW DO I PURSUE FAITH?

"In all this you greatly rejoice, though now for a little while you may have had to suffer grief in all kinds of trials. These have come so that the proven genuineness of your faith—of greater worth than gold, which perishes even though refined by fire—may result in praise, glory and honor when Jesus Christ is revealed."
1 Peter 1:6-7 NIV

When you accept Jesus as your Savior, you have faith. Period. Faith starts the moment you believe. However, if you want to increase your faith, that's another story. As we mentioned earlier, the whole idea of *Pursue Daily* is to help us pursue the gifts and qualities God has already given us through His Son, Jesus. If you're a believer, you have faith. It begins when you believe, but it's built and purified when you go through a trial.

1 Peter 1:6-7 tells us that we face trials so that our faith can be refined. Just like everything else, faith is built in time. The Bible talks about a spiritual gift of faith,[8] and some people are supernaturally gifted in this area. Still, the kind of faith 1 Peter is talking about is available to every believer in Christ, regardless if you are gifted with it or fighting for it.

If you want to pursue faith, be prepared to go through some storms. Faith is built when fear is buried. It's the whole "you have to go through the rain to get to the rainbow" logic. If you *really* want your faith to become great, then you will have to go through some things that will test and purify you.

Now, please don't get scared when I say this. Our God is a good God, and He does not create evil. He is good, and what He does is good.[9] He is light, and there is no darkness in Him.[10] Sometimes, however, He will allow us to walk through challenging moments to build our faith.

Consider learning to play the guitar. I am not a guitarist, but I have friends who are, so I'm living vicariously through them for this example. When you first start learning to play the guitar, your fingers and hands are often put into uncomfortable positions. Cramps happen. Then, when practicing chords, spots on your fingers start to become raw from the pressure of the guitar strings. Even though it hurts, you continue to practice your chords every day. Eventually, you form a callus on your fingers. This callus is a rough spot of skin that protects your fingers from the pain of the guitar strings, and those around you easily see these calluses. They're a token of your progress and allow to continue to move forward, playing the guitar unharmed.

Faith is like a callus building resilience for your soul. As you walk through difficult situations, your faith becomes stronger and stronger. As it strengthens, your faith allows you to continue to move forward without being broken down by guilt, shame, fear, or worry. Those around you will see the evidence of your faith through your peace and joy. The process of forming faith may not be the most fun, but the rewards of living life with the protection of faith are more than worth it.

So, friend, when facing a difficult situation, take it as an opportunity to pursue faith. James 1 says you should "consider it pure joy...whenever you face trials of many kinds, because you know that the testing of your faith produces perseverance."[11] As your faith grows, your perseverance grows. As your perseverance grows, your spiritual maturity grows,[12] transforming you into the likeness of Christ.

Daily Declaration

"I believe that when I was saved, I received faith. However, I make the decision today to pursue faith daily by trusting God in all circumstances. No matter what I face, I believe that God is working for my good, and in the end, He will strengthen my faith. I believe God only does good, and the enemy only does evil. Therefore, I put my trust and faith in God alone."

3

PURSUE RIGHTEOUSNESS

"So flee youthful passions and pursue righteousness, faith, love, and peace, along with those who call on the Lord from a pure heart."
2 Timothy 2:22 ESV

APPLE KNOWS APPLE

Any other Apple products people out there? *No, this is not an endorsement.* However, if you are an Apple user, you know the struggle of what I'm about to talk about.

When I got my first iPhone back in 2012 (when I was in ninth grade, might I add), I didn't understand the world I was being introduced to. Before long, my iPhone became my life. I found everything I wanted and needed there—social interaction, entertainment, safety, a way to stay connected to friends and family. Then, when I started college, I got a MacBook Pro. It was just like the iPhone, but in *laptop form*. My MacBook Pro and I had some good times together. It helped me complete online assignments, write papers, and keep track of my "diary." Then, when I graduated college and started working in full-time ministry, I got an Apple Watch to keep up with the flood of texts every Sunday morning. I even experienced the "phantom buzz" where I would feel my Apple Watch vibrate with a notification when I wasn't even wearing it! In short, before I knew it, I was 100% Team Apple.

I'll be honest. I do love Apple products. I love how everything is connected. I love how, when I get a text, I hear notifications from three different pieces of equipment in my house. I love that when I need to work on the go, I can pull up my documents from my laptop on my phone. I love that I feel like I'm always in the know.

However, what I *don't* love about Apple products is that the Apple store is the ONLY place you can officially go to get them repaired (unless you want to go off-roading). You either make an appointment and go to an Apple store, or you ship your valuable items to the nearest Apple store because, let's be honest, no one ever lives by an Apple store. It's always an ordeal to get there! However, despite my dislike of driving two hours to the Apple store, the Apple store is the best option to get my devices repaired because Apple is the company who created them in the first place. I'm willing to drive to the nearest store and pay an employee with a little Apple logo on her shirt to help me with my devices because no one knows Apple like Apple. Therefore, I trust them to help me with my Apple products.

You see, a lot of us take care of our products and devices by taking them to specialists who can repair them quickly and with the best knowledge possible to fix them. However, while we tend to do this with our possessions, we typically tend *not* to do this with our spirits and souls.

When something is "off" or "wrong," when the screen of our soul is cracked, or our spirit has dark spots, we tend to run to things like food, alcohol, work, shopping, drugs, relationships—you name it. All the while, our spirits and souls suffer because we refuse to take them to their original Creator for repairs. Just as no one knows Apple better than Apple, no one knows you better than God because God created you in His image.

WHAT IS RIGHTEOUSNESS?
"So flee youthful passions and pursue righteousness, faith, love, and peace, along with those who call on the Lord from a pure heart."
2 Timothy 2:22 ESV

I share this analogy with you about Apple because, to understand what righteousness is, we must understand who we are and who created us. I'm not going to lie—righteousness has always been a complex topic for me to grasp. However, when I read our theme verse for this chapter and saw that I was supposed to *pursue* righteousness, I had to learn more! So, let's look at righteousness together.

Righteousness, in the original Greek text (the first version of the Bible ever written) of 2 Timothy 2:22, was the word *dikaiosynē*.[1] This word, *dikaiosynē*, means the "state of him who is as he ought to be."[2] Another definition of this word is the "condition acceptable to God."[3] Righteousness can also mean integrity, virtue, purity, rightness, and correctness of thinking, feeling, and acting.[4] That's a lot of definitions, right?

Here's the good news. From all these definitions that describe the word "righteousness," we can piece together one definition that makes righteousness a tangible goal to pursue in our walk with God. When we put all these definitions together, we get this:

> *Righteousness is the state of being as one ought to be, which is acceptable to God because it is virtuous, pure, right, and correct.*

In short, righteousness means being in your original intended state. Did you know that the Bible says that God created you in His image?[5] Did you know God created you to be good, filled with integrity, virtue, purity, rightness, and correctness? When God created you, He created you with *good* in mind. However, due to the choice of Adam and Eve in Genesis 3 to disobey God, sin entered the world. As a result, every human being was corrupted with sin from that point on.

Sin affects everyone. The holiest person you can think of right now? Yeah, I hate to burst your bubble, but they struggle with sin. Why? Because salvation is not the *removal* of sin but rather an introduction to the grace that *redeems* all sin.

This introduction to grace is why salvation is essential; salvation is the act of God redeeming you back to your original intended state. God never intended for you to live in shame, guilt, or pain. God never intended for you to cling to worldly possessions or people for your fulfillment. God never intended you to be overcome with fear, anxiety, or depression.

John 10:10 says that Jesus came so we may have "life and life to the fullest!" And every time we choose to pursue righteousness, our good and right intended state created by God, we get closer and closer to *literally* living our best life.

WHY DO I NEED RIGHTEOUSNESS?

"For I tell you that unless your righteousness surpasses that of the Pharisees and the teachers of the law, you will certainly not enter the kingdom of heaven."
Matthew 5:20 NIV

We discussed that righteousness is the good, original state that God always intended for us. When we pursue it, we step closer to living the life God always wanted for us. In this section, though, we'll dive deeper into why we must pursue righteousness daily.

Our theme verse for this section, Matthew 5:20, captures a conversation conducted by Jesus. In this conversation, He says something very interesting about righteousness. According to Jesus Himself, righteousness is an essential attribute because we cannot enter the Kingdom of Heaven without it.[6]

Now, remember, before you start freaking out that you won't make it to heaven—all the topics we discuss in *Pursue Daily* are all characteristics that you receive automatically once you are saved. However, just because we have something doesn't mean we don't have to continue pursuing it. Therefore, we must still seek righteousness every day. Righteousness is a gift from God that comes through salvation.[7] How we steward that gift and live the best life possible here on earth while we're waiting for heaven is to put it to use.

At first glance, Matthew 5 may sound like Jesus is setting a high standard, saying to the people that if they're not as righteous as the "Pharisees" and "teachers of the law," they won't make it to heaven. On the contrary, this verse does not set a high standard at all. If you're like me, when I first read Matthew 5:20, I was like, "Oh man. I've got to be more righteous than my pastor? I've got to be more righteous than my dad? I've got to be more righteous than the Pope? Well, I might as well quit now." And back in the day when Jesus was delivering this teaching during His sermon, many people probably thought this way as well. However, if you know anything about Jesus's relationship with the Pharisees in the New Testament, this statement is, for lack of better terms, a massive slap in the face to the Pharisees.

Jesus couldn't *stand* the Pharisees. He thought they were a bunch of phonies (and they were). They would put on shows and pretend to love God for attention, but they didn't have a real relationship with Him.[8] I mean, the Son of God, the Messiah, the One they had been waiting for *for so long*, was right in front of them, and they didn't even know it. How well do you know someone if you don't recognize them when they're standing right in front of you? Jesus even called the religious leaders a "brood of vipers."[9] He wasn't afraid to tell them what He thought about them.

When Jesus told the crowd that their righteousness had to "surpass" the righteousness of the Pharisees, in all actuality, He wasn't setting a high standard at all. Jesus was portraying that it's not about the level of difficulty; it's about the level of intimacy. He was saying that it is *easy* to get into the Kingdom of Heaven as long as you have an intimate and real relationship with God. And let me just add here: **God wants it to be as easy as possible for people to enter His Kingdom.** 1 Timothy 2:3-4 says that God "wants everyone to be saved and to come to a knowledge of the truth," and Acts 15:19 tells us that we "should not make it difficult for [people] who are turning to God" to begin a relationship with Him. Why, then, would He make it nearly impossible for people to be saved?

He wouldn't.

One must be righteous to enter the Kingdom of Heaven, and that righteousness comes through salvation. However, while we're still here kickin' it on earth, we must pursue righteousness every day to have the life God always intended for us.

HOW DO I PURSUE RIGHTEOUSNESS?

"See, I set before you today life and prosperity, death and destruction...This day I call the heavens and the earth as witnesses against you that I have set before you life and death, blessings and curses. Now choose life, so that you and your children may live and that you may love the Lord your God, listen to His voice, and hold fast to Him."
Deuteronomy 30:15-20 NIV

As I mentioned earlier, the only thing that can make us righteous is having a relationship with Jesus. When Jesus was on the cross, He took all the dirt and grime for us so that we could be made shiny and new, coming to completion in the original state God always intended. If your question is, "How do I become righteous?" the answer is believing in Jesus! If your question is, "How do I *pursue* righteousness?" the answer is becoming like Jesus.

Righteousness, defined earlier in this chapter, is all things good, true, noble, right, pure, lovely, admirable, excellent, and praiseworthy, which are the things the Apostle Paul tells us to think about in Philippians 4.[10] If we want to pursue righteousness, we must make choices that result in righteousness. If we're going to pursue goodness, we must make good choices.

A few months ago, I thought about my future children (I do this quite often). Austin and I are not parents yet, but as I learn lessons from other parents and read parenting Scriptures in the Bible, I write them down for safekeeping until the day comes when I can put them to use. One morning, I thought about the phrase "make good choices." I had a teacher in high school who would say that every day when the bell rang while we were walking to our next class. I always admired her for saying that because, clearly, that phrase stuck with me for years to come.

However, as I started thinking about this phrase—"make good choices"—I realized something. "Good" is relative. Depending on where you grew up, what religion you're a part of, who raised you, etc., it's possible you could've been taught something was good when it was actually bad. There are things that the world deems "good" that are entirely against God's Word, and this is why I want to flip the script on this saying. As I was thinking and praying about it, the Holy Spirit dropped a new phrase into my heart: **Make God choices.**

Not make *good* choices.

Make *God* choices.

What is a "God choice"? It's a choice that will push us closer to righteousness. It's a choice that will lead us to good, holy things that God always intended for us. While it may be contrary to what the world is saying is "good," it's a choice that will ultimately bring heaven to earth. God choices align with the Word of God and, eventually, lead us to pursue righteousness.

How do we make God choices? It's very simple.

1. Identify the original state that God intended for you.
2. Make decisions that push you closer to that state.

Did you know God's Word has much to say about you? Did you know that God's Word is the greatest hype song you could ever have? If you've ever wondered why you exist and what you were born to do, I guarantee you can find it in God's Word. Don't believe me? I dare you to try it.

If you truly know what God's Word says about you, then you know the original state God intended for you! And if you know the state that God intended for you, then you'll know what decisions will push you closer to that state. Here are just a few Scriptures that speak to who God created you to be in Christ:

- A new creation (2 Corinthians 5:17)
- Appointed for a purpose (Jeremiah 1:5)
- One with God (1 Corinthians 6:17)
- A child of God (1 John 3:1)
- Compassionate, kind, humble, meek, and patient (Colossians 3:12)
- Blessed with every spiritual blessing and united with Christ (Ephesians 1:3)
- Redeemed and forgiven (Ephesians 1:7)
- A masterpiece (Ephesians 2:10)
- More than a conqueror (Romans 8:37)
- A chosen people, a royal priesthood, a holy nation, and God's special possession (1 Peter 2:9)

Consider these verses above, and then consider every decision as one of two pathways. One path leads to light, and one path leads to darkness. You can tell the difference between the two (because the lines can get blurred sometimes) by knowing what God's Word says about you and Him. The path aligned with Scripture leads to righteousness, purity, integrity, and goodness. The other path leads to sin, guilt, shame, and frustration.

When you're at a party, will you drink that or not? When you're hanging out with your friends, will you let things get out of hand or not? When you're at school, and someone's sitting alone, will you sit with them or not? When you're alone in your room late at night, will you watch that or not?

Every time you make a decision that is in favor of godliness, you are pursuing righteousness! Fall in love with God's Word, friends, and know what it says is good, right, pure, and lovely. Cling to those things and make God choices. With every decision you face, remember God's Word. Remember what He thinks and believes. Remember what He thinks about you. Choose the path of righteousness. With every God choice, you're getting closer and closer to the original state God intended for you, which is good, pleasing, and perfect.[11]

Daily Declaration

"I believe that God only wants what's best for me. I believe that God created me to be beautiful, right, just, and pure, but I also understand that I am a sinful person in need of a Savior. I know that through Jesus's sacrifice, I have been made righteous, and that is the only way I can become righteous. Therefore, as a result of Jesus's sacrifice, I choose to make God decisions that honor Him and push me towards all the good things He has in store for me."

4

PURSUE LOVE

"So flee youthful passions and pursue righteousness, faith, love, and peace, along with those who call on the Lord from a pure heart."
2 Timothy 2:22 ESV

THE FIRST KISS

It was a Thursday night. Everyone else had gone to bed. It was just Austin and me in the living room. A month ago, we never thought we'd be sitting here.

Austin and I started dating in February 2020, a few weeks before the COVID-19 pandemic hit the United States, and everything changed. I lived in Birmingham, Alabama, and Austin lived in Florida. We had met through a mutual friend in December and had connected again later that January. After three weeks of talking on the phone and FaceTiming, Austin bought a plane ticket and flew to Birmingham to ask my dad for permission to date me. That was a bold move. And it was attractive. Take notes, dudes.

We spent three days together, and in those three days, Austin asked me to be his girlfriend, he met my family, and I met his family. We built a lot of memories together, and Austin will tell you that it was on that trip, specifically during a conversation in a local donut shop eating a cinnamon roll the size of our faces, that he knew one day he'd marry me.

After our fairytale-esque weekend together, I dropped him off at the airport, not knowing when I'd see him again. He was going back to Florida. I was staying home in Birmingham, preparing to go to South Africa in a few weeks for work. Little did we know that the next three weeks would change our lives forever.

Austin returned to Alabama for a month during quarantine so he wouldn't have to stay at his apartment by himself. This trip also meant that, even though we were long-distance dating, we spent a month together. Earlier that month, Austin had told me he was in love with me, and here I was at his family's house in Huntsville for the second weekend, sitting with him on the couch.

I knew our first kiss was coming. I could feel it. As we sat on the couch, he looked at me and then looked away. He did this several times, and then he said, "Hey, you want to go outside for a bit?" Knowing what was coming, I thought, "Kissing outside is romantic. I'll take it." So I said, "Sure, why not?"

We walked out to his back porch. It was early spring, so a nice chill was in the air. We sat on a bench together. The moment was getting closer.

We sat in silence for a few minutes. Then Austin looked at me and asked the question I knew was coming: "May I kiss you?" (Take notes again, dudes. It goes a long way when you ask the girl for permission to put your lips on hers).

He took my breath away. I knew it was coming, but it was also so new and unexpected at the same time. I looked back at him, smiled, and said, "Yes."

This was it. The big moment.

Up until this point, I had never been kissed. *Never*. In fact, I had been so nervous about this moment that I had asked a lot of friends for advice on how to kiss someone. Everyone I asked said the same thing: "It just comes naturally. Do what feels natural in the moment." Okay, great. I can do that. I can be natural.

Austin started to lean in, and my mind was spinning with all the slow, dramatic first kisses I'd watched on TV and in movies. I was about to experience my very own! I couldn't believe it! And when Austin was about halfway to my lips, the unexplainable happened. It came naturally, so I did what was most natural for me at that moment.

He leaned in, and suddenly, I grabbed his arm and yelled, "Oh, God!"

He stopped.

"Excuse me?" he asked. I just stared at him. I couldn't believe I just yelled, "Oh, God!" as my first kiss was about to take place! What is wrong with me?!

"I'm sorry," I said back. "I'm just nervous. Keep going." He recalibrated and continued en route for my lips. "Don't say anything," I told myself. "Don't do anything." So, once again, I did what was natural for me in that moment.

He kissed me, and I did nothing.

Absolutely *nothing*.

Poor guy. It probably felt like kissing a 2x4 piece of wood that occasionally yells, "Oh, God!" when it's nervous.

Once again, Austin looked at me, and I said, "I'm sorry. Try again."

Here he goes for round two—and same thing. No movement. No puckering. No slow, dramatic first kiss like it's shown in the movies. Eventually, I did get the hang of it, and the rest is history! But my goodness, that first kiss was something else and nothing like what I'd thought it'd be.

Now, we have a great story to tell, and it's hilarious looking back on it. But in the moment, I was devastated. This was our first kiss! I loved him! Why didn't kissing come naturally to me? When you love someone, shouldn't acts of love come naturally to you?

Oof. That line of thought hit me like a ton of bricks.

You see, even though I love Austin, the acts of love don't always come naturally. Different things like exhaustion and emotions can sometimes blind the desire to put love into action, and when it comes to our relationships with God, it's the same thing. Even though we love Him, sometimes the acts of our love for Him don't always come naturally.

So, what do we do? We pursue love daily.

WHAT IS LOVE?

"So flee youthful passions and pursue righteousness, faith, love, and peace, along with those who call on the Lord from a pure heart."
2 Timothy 2:22 ESV

Our theme verse for this chapter is 2 Timothy 2:22, which tells us to pursue love. Now, before you drop this book and pick up the phone to call your crush, this verse is not telling us to pursue a romantic relationship. While there's nothing wrong with dating (hence the intro story), the kind of love we'll be talking about goes much deeper than that.

The New Testament talks about different forms of love. While I, as an English speaker, only have one word for "love," the New

Testament and its original authors had other Greek words for different versions of love. Here are some examples of the kinds of love we see in the Bible:

- Storge - family/blood-related love
- Philia - friendship love
- Eros - romantic love
- Agapē - unconditional "God" love

While it is essential to pursue love with your family, friends, and significant other, the kind of love 2 Timothy is telling us to pursue is *agapē,* the unconditional love of God. *Agapē* is "affection, goodwill, love, [and] benevolence."[1] As we discuss love together, we're talking about pursuing the affection, goodwill, love, and benevolence of God.

Let me say this before we go any further: **love is a choice.** Just as I thought my love expressed would come naturally with Austin, we often believe the same thing about our love for God. However, love takes work, and if you're scared about taking the leap to pursue God's love daily because you've been heartbroken in the past, remember this: **God chose to love us first**.

1 John 4:19 says, "We love because He (Jesus) first loved us." So, while pursuing love for your family, friends, or significant other may have left you feeling rejected, hurt, or less valuable, know that when you choose to love God, He will never push you away. In fact, because He made the first step, any time you choose not to love God, you're actually rejecting *Him.* He knows what it feels like to be rejected. He knows what it feels like to be hurt. He knows what it feels like to love someone who doesn't love Him back. And guess what? He still chooses to love us anyway. Despite all the "what ifs" and "could have beens," wouldn't it be great if we made the choice to pursue love?

WHY SHOULD I PURSUE LOVE?

"Jesus replied: 'Love the Lord your God with all your heart and with all your soul and with all your mind. This is the first and greatest commandment. And the second is like it: Love your neighbor as yourself. All the Law and the Prophets hang on these two commandments.'"
Matthew 22:37-40

Now that we've established that love is a choice, let's discuss why we should choose it. As we see from our theme verse for this section, Jesus gave us two commandments that everything else depends on—*everything*. And guess what both commandments have to do with? Love.

We must pursue love daily because we cannot obey God without choosing to love. Think about it—Jesus commands us to do two things: love God and love people. As our senior pastor says at our home church, you can't focus on following rules 109 or 135 "until you've learned how to follow rules one and two."[2] According to Matthew 22:37-40, the two most important rules are loving God and loving others.

If we focus on fixing every little detail of our lives, correcting every sin, and doing every good thing we know to do but choose not to love God and others, we miss the point.

Paul says it this way in 1 Corinthians 13:

"If I speak in the tongues of men or of angels, but do not have love, I am only a resounding gong or a clanging cymbal. If I have the gift of prophecy and can fathom all mysteries and all knowledge, and if I have a faith that can move mountains, but do not have love, I am nothing. If I give all I possess to the poor and give over my body to hardship that I may boast, but do not have love, I gain nothing."[3]

Without love, Paul says that the words we speak are empty, the actions we do mean nothing, and our very being doesn't add value to the world around us. Without the choice to love, we are nothing, and we gain nothing.

But what does it look like when we choose to pursue love daily? What does it look like when we choose to love God, love the people around us, and love ourselves? Yeah, I threw "love ourselves" in there, too, because the commandment is "love your neighbor as yourself."[4] If you don't know how to love yourself, how can you love the people around you?

Here are some verses we find in the Bible that highlight the power of choosing to pursue love:

- "Let love and faithfulness never leave you; bind them around your neck, write them on the tablet of your heart. Then you will **win favor** and **a good name** in the sight of God and man." (Proverbs 3:3-4)
- "Above all, love each other deeply, because **love covers over a multitude of sins**." (1 Peter 4:8)
- "There is no fear in love. But **perfect love drives out fear**, because fear has to do with punishment. The one who fears is not made perfect in love." (1 John 4:18)
- "Whoever pursues righteousness and love finds **life, prosperity, and honor**." (Proverbs 21:21)
- "Hatred stirs up conflict, but **love covers over all wrongs**." (Proverbs 10:12)
- "Instead, speaking the truth in love, we will **grow** to become in every respect the **mature body** of Him who is the head, that is, Christ." (Ephesians 4:15)

When we pursue love for God and the people around us, we win favor with God and create a good reputation. We look past sins and wrongdoings and find it easier to forgive. We are fearless, confident, and mature in every way. When we choose to pursue love daily, we become more like Jesus.

HOW DO I PURSUE LOVE?
"Whoever does not love does not know God, because God is love."
1 John 4:8 NIV

We've established what love is and why we need to pursue it. Now, it's time to discuss how we pursue love because, let's be honest, it's not always easy! Looking at this section's verse, we see two forms of love represented: love as a *noun* and love as a *verb*. Let's discuss each one briefly.

1 John 4:8 says that "God is love." God is *love*. God is *agapē*. Love is not just something He "does." It's not just a feeling, emotion, or choice He makes now and then. Love is *who He is*. It's His constant state. There will never be a day where our God is not love.

When it comes to people, though, it's a different story. We don't see anywhere in the Bible where the word "love" is used as a noun to represent people. That's what makes Him God and us human. However, God created us with the ability to love, put it into action, and express it to the rest of the world.

In the original Greek language of 1 John 4:8, the verb form of "love" is the word *agapaō*.[5] *Agapē* is who God is, but *agapaō* is what we, as humans, are called to do. *Agapaō* is the agapē love of God expressed to humanity and through humanity. *Agapaō* means "to welcome, entertain, be fond of, and love dearly."[6] Since *agapaō* is a verb, it means it's something we have to put into action. It's something that we must pursue daily and put into use. How do we *agapaō*?

Notice that 1 John 4:8 says, "Whoever does not love does not know God." It doesn't say, "Whoever does not love *God* does not know God." Instead, it says that if we don't know how to love *at all*, we don't really know our Creator. This revelation leads us to believe that *agapaō* wasn't just meant to be an expression of love towards God; it was also meant to be an expression of love towards people. Without loving God, we can't genuinely love people, and the reverse is also true. Without loving people, we can't truly love God. Therefore, we put *agapaō* into practice by welcoming, entertaining, being fond of, and dearly loving people daily.

Welcome People.

"Therefore welcome one another as Christ has welcomed you, for the glory of God." - Romans 15:7 ESV

In the original Greek language, "welcome" is another word for receive.[7] To welcome people is to receive or accept them for who they are, even if you don't approve of what they do. There is a difference between approval and acceptance. Approval says, "I validate what you do." Acceptance says, "I love who you are."

Even when you may not agree with people or approve of their beliefs or lifestyles, it is still possible to love them with *agapē* love. We decide to make them feel at home. We include them in conversations. We take care of their needs. We make them feel seen and heard. When we welcome people, we are putting *agapaō* into action.

Entertain People.

"Let each of you look not only to his own interests, but also to the interests of others." - Philippians 2:4 ESV

Good entertainment is identified by how well it can keep an audience's attention. I know if a movie is good by whether or not

I'm checking the time throughout the showing. I know if I'm having fun at a theme park by whether or not I'm counting down the hours until it's time to leave.

Entertainment and attention go hand-in-hand. When we choose to entertain people, we pay attention to them. We notice them. We listen to what they have to say instead of cutting them off so we can say what we want. We make sacrifices for them when they call or text us for help. We make time for them and their needs. When we entertain people and acknowledge their needs, *agapaō* prevails.

Value People.
"Do nothing out of selfish ambition or vain conceit. Rather, in humility value others above yourselves." - Philippians 2:3 NIV

When we choose to be fond of people, we value them. When choose to value people, we *add value* to them. Dr. John C. Maxwell has a book titled *25 Ways to Win with People: How to Make Others Feel like a Million Bucks*. When we value people, we make them feel like a million bucks!

Valuing people means finding something positive about every person we meet and telling them what we see. If we can't find anything positive, we speak to their potential by saying it to them prayerfully. We make every person we meet feel like a million bucks. When we value people, *agapaō* is shown.

Cherish People.
"Carry each other's burdens, and in this way you will fulfill the law of Christ." - Galatians 6:2 NIV

When we choose to cherish people, we love them dearly. We care about their situations. We care about their feelings. We understand that they are created by God with dignity and worth and treat them as such.

Dear love shares burdens. Before Austin and I got married, I remember talking with one of my best friends, Grace. She had gotten married the year before, and she married into a powerhouse family. Now, she was already a powerhouse of a woman! But I watched in awe as she handled the change of pace, publicity, and pressure of life with elegance and boldness.

Before I got married, I asked Grace what I should expect marrying a pastor because I knew marrying Austin meant taking on a higher spiritual responsibility, just like Grace had experienced. She responded:

"When you get married, the spiritual load will feel heavier for you, but it will feel so much lighter for Austin."

Why? Because Austin and I share each other's burdens. Yes, the spiritual weight of stepping into a new season was heavier for me, but I was able to take some of the pressure and weight off Austin. Because I love him, I don't care how heavy it feels; we are carrying this thing together!

It is important to point out here that Jesus says in Matthew 11:28, "Come to Me, all of you who are weary and carry heavy burdens, and I will give you rest." Burdens are not ours to carry forever; sometimes, however, we need help carrying our burdens to the feet of Jesus. When we share each other's burdens, we're not taking the spiritual weight of what others are going through and carrying it ourselves. We're simply helping them move the weight from their hearts to God's hands.

When we share each other's burdens, we love people dearly. We experience life with them. In good times, we rejoice with those who are rejoicing.[8] In bad times, we weep with those who are weeping.[9] In all times, we share each other's burdens and "obey the law of Christ,"[10] and we ultimately bring those burdens to Jesus in exchange for rest.[11] When we choose to cherish people and love this way, *agapaō* takes place.

Daily Declaration

"I know that God loves me. I understand that His love is the greatest love I could ever have, and because He decided to love me first, I can freely decide to love Him back. I know God has asked me to love Him and those around me. Therefore, I commit to loving God with all of my heart, soul, mind, and strength. I commit to loving my neighbor as myself. I will welcome, entertain, value, and cherish people from this day forward."

5

PURSUE PEACE

"So flee youthful passions and pursue righteousness, faith, love, and peace, along with those who call on the Lord from a pure heart."
2 Timothy 2:22 ESV

FALSE ALARM

When Austin and I first moved to Florida, I worked from home. Every day, I would set up my workspace in our home office and get to work, looking at the trees, birds, and sunlight from our windows. One day, Austin was at work, and I was home typing away. We had recently moved into a new home, and our neighborhood was small and quiet–just how we like it. We're well under the median age of the community, and there were rarely disturbances. I always felt safe at home, even if I was alone.

This day was the first time in a long time I had been working by myself at the house. Austin went through a season where he also worked at home, so I was used to having some companionship throughout the day. This particular day was bright and sunny. The weather was perfect outside. I could hear children laughing and playing out in the neighbor's yard. There were birds everywhere. I was doing my work, minding my own business, when suddenly, I heard something rattling.

I looked around to see what was moving, and I couldn't see anything. I then looked up and saw that my ceiling fan was shaking. "That's weird," I thought. "I didn't have that thing turned on."

As I was sitting there, analyzing the fan, I noticed that the window started shaking. At this point, I had no clue what was happening, but I felt deep in my being that I was about to die.

Okay, that's a little dramatic. But it's how I felt.

I grabbed my phone and called Austin while researching, "Does Florida have earthquakes?" I only reached his voicemail. I looked at a map on Google and saw no fault lines under Florida, so I assumed it wasn't an earthquake. Possibility number one was ruled out.

I called Austin again, but still no answer.

I remember being a kid in Mississippi and feeling my friend's house shake once. I thought that was an earthquake, too, but it turns out it was a meth lab that blew up in the woods behind our neighborhood. So, I thought, "Maybe something just exploded."

I looked outside the window (which was still rattling), and I didn't see any smoke or fire. Possibility number two was ruled out.

About this time, I heard a loud smash. It sounded like someone threw a chair against our window. And with that, I bolted for the guest bathroom at the center of the house. The only logical explanation was that someone was trying to break into our home, and I was not about to be caught in the open.

Once secured in the guest bathroom bathtub with the door locked, I called Austin for the third time, and finally, he picked up. Emphatically, I told Austin that someone was trying to break into our house.

"Whoa, slow down. Are you okay? What are you talking about, Emily? It's the middle of the day. Our neighborhood is quiet."

"I know, Austin, but I promise, someone just threw something at our window! And the ceiling fan was shaking too, so I think they're trying to come in from the roof!"

"That's ridiculous, Emily." He said. "What all happened?"

"Well, I was sitting in the office, and suddenly, the ceiling fan and window started shaking. I thought it was an earthquake, but we don't have those here. I checked. Then, I heard a loud smash and ran out of the office and locked myself in the guest bathroom."

"Oh, was it a rocket?"

A rocket?

You see, Austin and I bought a house near Cape Canaveral, the home of Kennedy Space Center, where NASA and SpaceX do some of their rocket launches. And that day, I discovered that when those rockets break the sound barrier, the sonic boom can be heard (and felt) at our house.

There I was, a sorry little puddle of an anxious mess because I thought someone was breaking into our house through the roof, only to find out that there had been a rocket launch a few miles from us. I was embarrassed but also amazed.

I was amazed that I could see and feel rocket launches from our house. I was embarrassed at how quickly a figment of my imagination ruined my quiet, peaceful, productive day. I allowed my emotions to get the best of me and wasn't operating out of peace. I was operating out of fear.

WHAT IS PEACE?

"So flee youthful passions and pursue righteousness, faith, love, and peace, along with those who call on the Lord from a pure heart."
2 Timothy 2:22 ESV

The word "peace" is used frequently in Christian jargon, but what exactly is peace? We hear it all the time in the Christian circuit. "I had peace about it, so…" or "I didn't have peace about it, so…" What is this "peace" that everyone is so enamored with and convinced of its benefits?

While peace can be a feeling, peace is more than a feeling. Our theme verse for this section tells us to pursue peace, along with other qualities. The original Greek word for peace in this verse is *eirēnē*,[1] which has a long list of definitions.

Here are just a few:

- National tranquility
- Peace between individuals (harmony)
- Security and safety
- The Messiah's peace (salvation)[2]

While all of these definitions are good to know (and VERY true), there's one definition that stands out from the rest as the *true* definition of the kind of peace Paul was talking about in 2 Timothy:

Eirēnē: The tranquil state of a soul assured of its salvation through Christ, and so fearing nothing from God and content with its earthly lot, of whatsoever sort that is.[3]

Peace is the state of being assured of your salvation and fearing nothing because you have the hope of heaven. When you have the hope of heaven, whatever life looks like on this earth, you're okay with it because you know that, at the end of the day, heaven is your home.

Paul writes in Philippians 3:20 that "our citizenship is in heaven," meaning that we don't belong to this world anymore whenever we are saved. This world doesn't own us or tell us what to do or how to live. We follow a higher calling, a Higher Power, and His name is Jesus. Now, that doesn't mean that we don't follow the rules or laws or respect authority; on the contrary, God's Word says a lot about being an excellent earthly citizen. But, for the purposes of peace, we must choose to identify ourselves not as a citizen of a country but as a citizen of God's heavenly Kingdom.

Peace is all about a heavenly perspective. Peace is a state of being that we can experience regardless of what we're going through or facing. Instead of focusing on the situation, we must change our perspective and focus on peace. Peace is the assurance that everything will be okay because God's got it.

Even if the situation isn't peaceful, we still can be peaceful. Why? Because peace isn't situational. Peace is eternal, and as we learn why we need peace and how we get peace, we can live in a constant state of heaven-on-earth by resting assured that God has our back in every situation.

WHY DO I NEED PEACE?
"And the peace of God, which transcends all understanding, will guard your hearts and your minds in Christ Jesus."
Philippians 4:7 NIV

As I mentioned earlier, peace is all about perspective. How many of you know a positive perspective takes work? Most humans don't naturally have a good attitude. It's not how we were wired— remember, sinful beings? We need a Savior like Jesus because we're naturally hopeless at doing or being anything good on our own. And when it comes to peace, we need Jesus's help because choosing it on our own is nearly impossible, especially since we established that *true* peace only comes from salvation in Jesus.

We have to pursue peace daily because it's a constant choice that we have to make. It's a continuous shift in perspective that we must choose. But why is it worth it? Why is it worth the constant perspective adjustment? Well, I'm glad you asked.

You see, we need peace for two reasons: peace is a guard, and peace is a guide.

Our Guard

We need to pursue peace because it's a guard for us. Our theme verse for this section, Philippians 4:7, says that peace protects our hearts and minds through Christ Jesus (who the Bible says is the Prince of Peace).[4] Our hearts and minds are the center of our thoughts, feelings, and relationships. There can be a lot that goes on in those areas! Without the guard of peace, we may wander into scenarios and situations that could harm us in multiple ways. Our hearts could get attached to people or things that we shouldn't be attached to. Our minds could imagine fantasies or create thought patterns that are irrational and unhealthy. However, when we pursue peace, we seek the guard to keep us safe and steady.

Our Guide

The second reason we need to pursue peace is that it's a guide for us. Check out this verse in Luke 8:48: "Then He (Jesus) said to her, 'Daughter, your faith has healed you. Go in peace.'" When reading this verse, I used to think that Jesus was giving peace to her as a blessing, saying to "walk away feeling peaceful." However, I found something exciting when I looked up the original meaning of the word "go" in this verse. "Go" in this context means to "pursue the journey."[5] Wow! There's our word!

At this moment, Jesus was telling this woman to *literally* pursue the direction of peace. This phrase means that when she faced a hard decision or had to pick a path, He commanded her to choose the result that would end in peace.

There may be many things to base our decisions on—money, fame, worldly values, peer pressure, popularity. However, God calls us to use the standard of peace to make choices. Just think about it: How much easier would your life be if every decision you made was based on whether it would result in peace? With peace as a guide, we can make better decisions that result in God's sovereignty and protection.

HOW DO I PURSUE PEACE?

"Do not be anxious about anything, but in every situation, by prayer and petition, with thanksgiving, present your requests to God. And the peace of God, which transcends all understanding, will guard your hearts and your minds in Christ Jesus."
Philippians 4:6-7 NIV

Knowing all this information about peace, how do we get closer to this "guard" and "guide" that will protect and lead our souls? If you read the verse for this section, you'll see that it is straightforward. We pursue peace daily through prayer. In fact, when pursuing peace, Paul outlines *precisely* what our prayer time is supposed to look like in Philippians 4! Let's look at how we pursue peace through prayer together.

We pray.

The original text for the word "prayer" means a "prayer addressed to God."[6] First and foremost, Paul writes that we are supposed to pray directly to God. The keyword in that sentence is *first*. This means that when something happens, or you're just DYING to tell someone about something you saw or heard, guess who gets to listen to it first? Not your BFF, parents, or sibling. God gets to hear it first! If you want to know what pursuing peace looks like, we can sum it up in this phrase: God always has first dibs. Period.

Something incredible happens when we decide to pray first and tell God about our problems or emotions before we allow them to reach someone else's ears. God is the perfect filter because He's wise, gracious, and always right. If you're wondering if you should really be upset about something, ask God first. If you're wondering if you should be worried about something, ask God first. As we choose to seek God first and address our prayers to Him, we begin the pursuit of peace.

We petition.

This one may be my favorite step of all! Paul not only says that we can pursue peace "by prayer," but he also says we can pursue peace by "petition."[7] Now, if you're anything like I was a year ago, the word "petition" can be tricky to understand. Depending on the translation you read of the Bible, that word can be replaced with "supplication." If anyone knows what supplication is, please let me know.

Since the word in our current translations can change, we need to look at the original text again to find the original meaning of the word. In this verse, the original Greek word "petition" or "supplication" means "seeking, asking, [or] entreating."[8] It means to pursue God and keep asking fervently.

Petitioning reminds me of Matthew 7:7, which says, "Ask and it will be given to you; seek and you will find; knock and the door will be opened to you." How effective would a knock be at a door if it only happened once? Do you know anyone who only knocks once? Probably not. Why? Because only one knock wouldn't get anyone's attention. It would be stifled by a loud air conditioner or mistaken for an item falling off a counter. However, when there are multiple knocks on the door, it gets someone's attention, and they know someone's waiting for them. It's the same way with God.

Now, God knows where you are all the time, so it's not like He's forgotten about you or doesn't know you exist. However, when we petition by praying constantly, He can't help but pay attention to our prayers. If you have a prayer request that you need God to answer, pray about it *constantly*. Keep knocking on the door, and I promise He'll answer.

Another way to think about "petition" is to think of a literal petition. A petition lists the names of individuals who come together to see change happen. When someone wants to see change on a higher level, they know that if they go there alone, they won't have much effect. However, if that person has two million people backing them up with signatures on a petition, then people start to take notice. Again, it's the same thing with God.

When we're pursuing peace through prayer, we must have people praying with us. The more people we have praying with us, the more names we have on our spiritual petition. The more names we have on our spiritual petition, the more power there is! Jesus says in Matthew 18:20, "Where two or three gather in my name, there am I with them." As we petition God with other people, His Word promises He will be there, too. I don't know about you, but I want God to show up in my prayers!

We praise.

On top of prayer and petition, Paul throws into the list that we must present requests to God "with thanksgiving."[9] Just because this phrase is the last on the list doesn't make it less powerful. Psalm 100:4 says that praise and thanksgiving are actually how we enter into the presence of God! When we give thanks and praise God, we are pursuing peace because we're reminded of how good of a God He is.

At this point, you might be thinking, "Well, why should I thank God? Why should I praise Him? My prayer hasn't even been answered yet!" And this is where the key to pursuing peace comes in: Peace is not a product of proof but a product of prayer. Let me say it this way: Peace does not come when you see the prayer answered; peace comes in the act of prayer itself.

So, you haven't seen any results yet? So, you've been praying for years and haven't received an answer yet? Give thanks. Praise God, even if it hasn't happened yet. There is power in thanking God for something before it happens! We have to find a Bible verse and say, "God, even though I haven't seen you move in this area yet, I thank you that Your Word says _____, and I thank you that you are moving!"

Even when you don't see, and even when you don't understand, praise God and thank Him anyway. He's moving on your behalf!

Life can be hard sometimes. Jesus told us it would be.[10] However, no matter our circumstances, we can have peace through Jesus! Whatever it is that you're anxious or fearful about, or whatever is bringing a disturbance to your peace, I encourage you to do three things:

1. Write down what's bothering you. Like, *everything*.

2. Find a Bible verse for each situation and speak it over yourself every day.
3. Thank God in advance for what He's going to do in each area.

God's Word promises that once you pray, petition, and praise, "the peace of God, which transcends all understanding, will guard your hearts and your minds in Christ Jesus."[11] When we make time to seek God first, gather a group of people to pray with us, and praise Him for the results, even when we don't see them yet, we are in a state of assurance—a state of peace.

Daily Declaration

"I believe peace is always readily available to me because of what Jesus did on the cross. From this point forward, I refuse to let worry, anxiety, or fear ruin my life. I will be bold, praying, petitioning, and thanking God whenever something tries to steal my peace. I know that God loves me and is able and willing to give me peace that surpasses all understanding—and when I do have peace, I will praise God because I know it's from Him."

6

PURSUE PURITY

"Flee the evil desires of youth and pursue righteousness, faith, love and peace, along with those who call on the Lord out of a pure heart."
2 Timothy 2:22 NIV

THE PIZZA PALACE

The location was some small, rundown pizza restaurant in the middle of nowhere in Mississippi. The date was March 2011. The time was 9:00 p.m. I was in the seventh grade, and my class took a "Tour of Mississippi" trip as our yearly excursion.

I know what you're thinking.

"What's there to tour in Mississippi?"

I'm still trying to figure that out, too.

The long bus rides through my home state were mixed tours of old homes, museums, parks, trails, and restaurants. Each destination had its dose of Mississippi-ness, meaning there was a lot of fried food, southern hospitality, and blues music. While the trip was enjoyable, there was a lot of history, artifacts, and lessons for a group of seventh graders. So, when we had the chance, we tried to shake things up and have some fun.

This night at the Pizza Palace in the middle of nowhere was the perfect time to have that fun. We ordered our pizza and sat at a table by the drink machine. I walked over to get water connected to the Coke outlet. As I pushed down the tab for water, I noticed it was coming out as a dark, muddy color. I stopped pushing down the lever and threw out the water.

"Let's try this again," I thought.

I pushed down the lever, and again, dark, murky water filled my cup. At this point, I was thirsty and ready for pizza, so I accepted the polluted water and went to sit back at my table.

Despite my hesitation, I took a sip of "water." Not too bad. The worker delivered our pizza to the table, and we started to eat. We were cracking jokes, playing pranks on each other—all the things that seventh graders do when they're allowed to eat dinner at 9:00 at night. I watched my friends "steal" pieces of pizza and take funny pictures of each other with their iPod touches as they ate. We were having a great time enjoying our food, each other's company, and the fact that we were at a pizza restaurant after the past few days of fried food and ham sandwiches.

Eventually, I got up to go to the bathroom. I was gone for a few minutes, and when I returned to the table, the laughing and joking was over. No one was saying anything. No one was eating. Everyone was just sitting in silence. Staring. At me.

I sat down and asked my friend Jade what was wrong. She shrugged it off and told me not to worry about it. I glanced at the restaurant, and nothing seemed to be off. Our chaperones were at a table across the way, eating and talking, so if they weren't concerned, I wouldn't be, either. There was still a piece of pizza on my plate, and I decided to eat it.

Everyone watched me.

And that's when it hit me.

"They're pranking me," I thought. "They put something on my pizza."

I picked up my slice and examined it carefully. No issues found. I looked at the pizza and then looked around the table. They were still staring. No sign of mischief. Just anticipation.

I thought long and hard about what I was about to do. Should I eat this slice of pizza? What did they do to it?

Finally, the growling of my stomach convinced me to take a bite. I did, and there was nothing wrong. It was just like every other piece of pizza I'd eaten, so I finished my slice. Then, I reached for my water. Yes, the murky water that the drink machine so graciously gifted me. I took a sip, and the entire table erupted.

"I can't believe you just did that!"

"How could you drink that?!"

My friends met me with all kinds of exclamations. I put the glass down and looked at it. All I saw was murky water! All I tasted was murky water! I drank it again, and another round of gasps and screams occurred.

"Emily, stop that! We were just joking!"

I was confused at this point, so I looked at Jade and asked her what was wrong. Through spurts of laughter, she informed me that she and a couple of other friends had added some "special ingredients" to my drink while I was in the bathroom. Things like parmesan cheese, red pepper flakes, and a straw wrapper.

I sat in disbelief. I couldn't see or taste any of the things they had put in my drink, which led me to question just how murky the water was in the first place. I got up to pour out my water, and, sure enough, chunks of *all kinds* of things fell out of my cup. I couldn't believe that I had drunk that! How did I not know that all that nasty stuff was in my drink?

Isn't it funny how sometimes things become so dark and murky that we can't tell what's good or bad anymore? I was drinking water that—first and foremost—was not clean. As I drank it, I got used to its flavor, and then, when my friends added other gross things to it, I didn't even notice.

This story is an excellent representation of what impurity can look like in many of our lives. We start with something that we think is harmless, but the more we use it, look at it, or do it, the more we get used to it. Then, when harmful things do come into play, we can't even recognize them because we've already blinded ourselves by the darkness we allowed in the first place.

This progression of contamination is why purity is such a big deal. It keeps us from falling into evil, dark, and unclear things. As we discuss pursuing purity in this chapter, I want you to remember a few things:

We will discuss some things in this chapter that are PG-13, and there's nothing to be afraid of.

I'm just going to be honest: there's no way that we can talk about purity without at least mentioning sex. And before we even begin the conversation, I need you to know that sex is not something that is "evil" or "awful." Sex, along with our bodies and purity, are incredible gifts from God that, when stewarded well, can be used for enjoyment, fulfillment, and, ultimately, to glorify the Lord. So, put on your big girl pants. We're not pulling punches.

Impurity, whether by choice or by force, can be restored.

Some of us have made poor decisions in our lives, and some of us must live with the ramifications of someone else's poor choices.

Whether impurity has entered your life by choice or force, God can restore your purity.

I'm not a professional in this area. However, there are professionals in this area who love Jesus, and I know they would love to help you, too.

I will do my best to teach you God's Word on this topic. However, I don't have all the answers. At any point in this chapter, if things start to come up that you realize need additional professional attention, don't feel guilty. Asking for help from a licensed counselor or mental health therapist doesn't mean that you don't trust God or His Word. Asking for help is brave! God is the one who gave us doctors, counselors, and psychologists in the first place, so it's okay to seek professional help in your pursuit of purity if needed.

Now, let's dive in!

WHAT IS PURITY?

"Flee the evil desires of youth and pursue righteousness, faith, love and peace, along with those who call on the Lord out of a pure heart."
2 Timothy 2:22 NIV

Contrary to popular belief, purity goes far beyond one's sexual status. Purity, in 2 Timothy, means to be clean or pure "physically," in a "Levitical" (or spiritual) sense, and "ethically."[1] In other words, purity pertains to the **body** (the physical), **spirit** (the spiritual), and **soul** (the ethical). To be biblically pure, we must be clean in every area of our lives.

One way to understand purity is to know what purity is not. The modern definition of purity is "the freedom from adulteration or contamination."[2] This definition means that *impurity* is anything that brings adulteration or contamination into our lives.

Adulteration is the action of making something poorer in quality by the addition of another substance.[3] Think of the word "adultery." Adultery occurs when one person from a married relationship engages in sexual relations with someone other than his/her spouse. Marriage is a sacred institution; it is holy and made up of two people: a man and a woman. However, when one of the people in the marriage commits adultery, he/she adds another person to the mix, making the marriage less than holy. In the same way, adulteration in our lives can come in the form of substances, addictions, thoughts, actions, and emotions. These less-than-perfect items can enter our being, our design, which God says is fearfully and wonderfully made,[4] and when added to us, they destroy our purity.

Purity is also freedom from contamination. Contamination is the action or state of making or being made impure by polluting or poisoning.[5] Unfortunately, the sad thing about contamination is that we often don't know that something is causing pollution until after it happens. Here's an illustration to prove this point.

The first gasoline-powered car was invented in America in 1893. However, it wasn't until the early to mid-1900s that people began using them regularly, especially in large cities like New York City. Around that time, officials started to notice an enormous public health crisis in the cities. People were getting sick and dying quite frequently. In due time, the health officials discovered the culprit of the problem: pollution.

They discovered that as cars burned fuel, carbon monoxide was produced, and that substance was so heavily prevalent in the cities because of the rise of personal transportation. Consistently exposed to carbon monoxide, people got it in their bloodstream, which caused carbon monoxide poisoning. That poisoning resulted in symptoms such as headaches, nausea, vomiting, dizziness, and, if left untreated, death. Thankfully, in 1970, the government passed the Clean Air Act, which allowed the EPA to regulate the pollution from cars and other modes of transportation. Therefore, the carbon monoxide we are exposed to today from fuel emissions is incredibly less than in the mid-1900s.

Even so, let's go back to 1893. It is plausible to think that the inventors of the first car never intended to pollute the earth. It is also conceivable to believe that they never intended to poison people through pollution. However, it wasn't until nearly *70 years after* they invented the gasoline-powered car that the effects of the pollution were seen, and the most noticeable impact of the pollution was poison.

You see, contamination exists when both pollution and poison are present. Just as the inventors of the gasoline-powered car did not know the effects it would have on the human population until later, there are things we allow into our lives that we won't see the repercussions from until we're older. Things like pornography, drinking, listening to music with inappropriate lyrics, etc., may not seem harmful now, but when you open yourself up to things that are not pure or holy, you allow pollution to enter your life. This pollution leads to poison, which ultimately, if left untreated, leads to death. These things may not lead to physical death, but they could lead to the death of our dreams, joy, peace, and every good thing God has created.

So, we've talked a lot about impurity, but let's define purity. Purity is the freedom from adulteration and contamination. It's freedom from adding things into our lives that will reduce our quality of life. It's freedom from pollution and poisoning. It's a clean and pure state in the body, soul, and spirit. Purity isn't a set of rules to be followed; purity is *freedom*.

WHY DO I NEED PURITY?

"Blessed are the pure in heart, for they will see God."
Matthew 5:8 NIV

In what is penned as Jesus's most famous sermon, the Sermon on the Mount, Jesus tells us that the pure in heart are blessed because they will see God. In the original Greek language of the New Testament, the word "see" means to "know [and] become acquainted with through experience."[6] It's one thing to know *about* God by listening to messages and podcasts, reading books, and reading your Bible. It's another thing to *know* God personally through experience. In Matthew 5, Jesus tells us that those who experience God are those who are pure.

We need to pursue purity because, through purity, we get to experience the most of God! In the Old Testament, there was something called a tabernacle. This tabernacle was the place where people entered the presence of God. There were very few "worship nights" or "prayer meetings" outside of the tabernacle because the tabernacle is where God's Spirit dwelled. Therefore, people had to go to the tabernacle to be in God's presence. However, they couldn't just waltz in at any time or any way they wanted. A strict protocol had to be followed for them to be in the presence of God. This protocol was one of cleansing—physically, emotionally, and spiritually—and it had to occur before they could enter God's presence because He could not come into contact with something (or someone) unclean.

Think of getting a fresh, new pair of white sneakers. They come in a box that's never been opened. The shoes are in plastic bags inside the box and have paper stuffed to keep the desired shape. The laces are crisp. There are no scuff marks anywhere on the shoes. The soles of the shoes don't have a hint of dirt on them. They are *perfect*.

Then, picture some socks. These socks were just on your feet as you ran through a massive mud puddle in your front yard, trying to get the garbage can out on the road before the garbage truck made it to your house (I'm *totally* not speaking from personal experience…). Picture taking the new, crisp white shoes out of the box and putting them on your wet, muddy sock feet. Gross, right? You would never do that! Why? Because the socks are dirty, and the shoes are perfect. You wouldn't allow your dirty socks to touch your perfect shoes!

In the same way, our sin and dirtiness cannot be combined with God's perfection. Don't get me wrong—there is nothing we can do to contaminate or harm God's purity because He's God. However, God cannot bless something impure, and when we try to enter His presence unclean, we can't.

Now, thank God for Jesus because, through His sacrifice, we have been made clean and now have full access to God anytime![7] However, as we've mentioned in the chapters before, just because we have something doesn't mean we don't have to pursue it. Yes, we are pure, but we must continue making choices that protect our purity. This pursuit of purity is sometimes referred to as "progressive sanctification," which means that we are progressively sanctified (becoming holy) throughout our lives.[8] Therefore, we must think about our bodies, souls, and spirits and how we can stay clean in all areas. As we continue to remain pure and allow God to cleanse us, we experience more and more of Him.

HOW DO I GET PURITY?

"How can a young person stay on the path of purity? By living according to Your word."
Psalm 119:9 NIV

As we mentioned a few sentences ago, if you have a relationship with Jesus, you automatically possess purity. You have purity because when Jesus died on the cross, His death was a sacrifice for your atonement.[9] Atonement is a biblical word for "settling the score." In the Old Testament, any time someone had sinned, they would have to sacrifice an animal as an atonement for their sins. The animal's blood would, in a sense, "cover" their mistake, and all would be well with God—until the next mess-up happened and yet another sacrifice had to be made.

However, Isaiah wrote to Israel, God's chosen people, that "though [their] sins be like scarlet, they shall be as white as snow."[10] The phrase "shall be" indicated that one day in the future, God would forgive the peoples' sins completely without atonement being needed every time they sinned. This "one day" was a direct reference to the crucifixion and resurrection of Jesus. Today, as believers, we live under the atonement of what Jesus did on the cross for us. Hebrews 9 discusses the process of this atonement, stating that "Christ was sacrificed once to take away the sins of many."[11] Through the shedding of His blood on the cross, we have been made clean, pure, and holy.[12]

So, if you thought there'd never be a way to be pure again, worry not! As a believer in Jesus, you *are* pure. However, purity is something that we must continue to choose every day because almost everything we are exposed to is trying to taint our purity.

What we hear on the radio or various streaming services.
What we see on Netflix.
What we see on social media.
What we see in the news.
What we hear from celebrities, politicians, and all the people who have the most prominent platforms.

And if we're not careful, we'll allow these sources to speak to us more than God's Word, which is how Psalm 119:9 says we stay pure. Let's look at three important points from Psalm 119:9.

Purity is a path.

Purity is more than a state of being or a label we put on ourselves or others. One of my favorite TV shows of all time is *Gilmore Girls*. When I think about purity as a label, I often think about when Tristan calls Rory "Mary" during their time together at Chilton Academy. He called her "Mary" in reference to the Virgin Mary since Rory was so pure.

Incidentally, her purity became her identity; it became her label. And while there's nothing wrong with being known as a "pure" person (I hope we all desire that!), there is something wrong with only seeing purity as a status. Because when that status is lost, your purity is as well.

I recently realized I had always associated purity with virginity. If you're not married, it is not a bad thing to be a virgin. God desires for sex to be an incredible experience shared between a husband and wife in the context of marriage. However, when you convince yourself that being pure means being a virgin, then one day, when you're not one anymore, even if you're in a healthy marriage, you may feel dirty or unclean.

The vital thing to note is that purity is not a label; purity is a *path*. Better yet, purity is a *lifestyle*. It encompasses more than our sexual status. Can I say something that may blow your mind? It's possible to be a virgin and yet still be impure. You can be a virgin but still struggle with overeating. You can be a virgin but still have a potty mouth. You can be a virgin but still watch and listen to things that corrupt your soul.

And you want to know something else? You could not be a virgin and *still be pure*. Friend, you could have made a poor decision in your past. Someone could have made a poor decision that involved you and corrupted your innocence, and just because you're not a "virgin" in the world's eyes doesn't mean you can't be pure.

In Revelation 21, Jesus says He is "making all things new."[13] And "all things" include *you*. Whatever choices you've made or life experiences you've had, know that purity is still possible with God. A status or label does not determine purity; it's determined by a pursuit of a holy lifestyle with Jesus.

The only way to stay pure is to live by God's Word.

Now that we know purity is a path, let's talk about how we stay on course. According to Psalm 119:9, the only way a young person (and I would add *anyone*) can stay pure is by living by God's Word. In the original text, the phrase "living by" means "to keep, guard, observe, give heed."[14] This phrase shows that to live a life of purity, we must learn God's Word and then hold onto what we know. At the end of the day, opinions don't matter—including our own. When we live according to God's Word, we take our lives and line them up to what we read in the Bible. We test ourselves and our lifestyle against what is written in God's Word. We "keep" and "guard" ourselves by placing the boundaries the Bible sets for us.

It deeply saddens me that people have become accustomed to getting information and advice from everywhere other than the Bible. A recent study conducted by the Barna Group shows that teenagers in the United States trust family and themselves more than they trust the Bible to learn more about Jesus.[15] While the same study shows that 95% of teenagers who are Christians view the Bible as the ultimate source of truth,[16] it also saddens me that people who do see the Bible as truth live in constant confusion about what's right and what's wrong in Scripture. In today's world, especially when it comes to hot topics like homosexuality, abortion, immigration, etc., the world and the Church cannot seem to agree (which is not surprising). However, what's immensely puzzling is that the Church can't seem to agree with itself! With so much confusion and chaos surrounding God's Word within the Church, how are we supposed to know what's right? How are we supposed to know what to live by?

I think the answer is quite simple. **If God really is God, then His Word really is His Word**. Here's what I mean by this statement: If God really is the God who created the heavens and the earth and who runs everything and knows everything and sees everything, then surely, He's powerful enough to assure that what He meant to be in His Word is in there, just as He wants it to be.

All the chaos and confusion over "interpretations" and "versions" makes my heart hurt. So many people think God would allow His Word to be tainted in some way, shape, or form through the translating process, so much so that they believe the Bible we're reading today isn't His "actual Word." I'll be honest; I don't understand everything in the Bible. I don't know what the Bible says about every little thing. I haven't memorized every verse or chapter or word. But here's what I do know: God is the same—yesterday, today, and forever,[17] and if He is the same, then surely His Word must be the same, too.

That said, when you decide *for yourself* that the Word of God is accurate, powerful, and true, you can follow it as the path of purity. Following your favorite Christian celebrities or preachers on Instagram is fine. Listening to messages and podcasts is fine. Even reading books like the one you're reading right now is fine! However, none of these things compare to God's Word, and none of them can *replace* the role of God's Word in your life. The Bible is the only "true north" we have and is the only way to live a life of purity.

You can't live by the Word if you don't know the Word.

Chapter 1 discussed the importance of reading your Bible as a foundation of faith. The Word of God is a solid rock on which you can build your faith, but it is also the tool you need to go deeper in your relationship with the Lord and live the life God always intended for you.

You can't live by the Word unless you know the Word, and the only way to know it is to read it. This may surprise you because I'm a writer, but I used to *hate* reading. It was always my lowest grade in school. Always my lowest score in standardized testing. I hardly ever did it for fun and dreaded it when I had to do it for school. So, when it came to reading God's Word, I was scared. I thought I would dread it and receive an "F" on my ability to comprehend it. However, when I realized that reading God's Word wasn't a chore or graded assignment, I began to enjoy it. Sure, it took some time, but it became so much fun! The most enjoyable part was that I could physically see how it changed my life. The process of conviction and correction wasn't always fun, but it was what I needed, and the pain in the moment was completely worth the victory on the other side.

Just like I found a way to love reading the Bible, I believe you can have an incredible experience reading God's Word. You just have to find what works best for you. If you don't know where to start, begin in the Book of John. If you don't know when to read, try setting aside 15 minutes after you wake up every morning. If you don't know how to access the Bible, get a paper one or use an app on your phone. If you need a verse for a specific topic, search the topic online and then add "bible verses" at the end of it. There are so many ways to introduce God's Word into your everyday life, and trust me—when you do, you'll be blown away by how incredible it is to know and live by God's Word.

Daily Declaration

"I believe I am pure through Jesus Christ. Regardless of my past, present, or future mistakes, I know that Jesus forgives me and has made me new. I am no longer polluted or contaminated by the things of this world. I will not allow things into my life that push me further from God. Instead, I choose to pursue the path of purity by learning God's Word and living by God's Word."

7

PURSUE HUMILITY

"In the same way, you who are younger, submit yourselves to your elders. All of you, clothe yourselves with humility toward one another, because, 'God opposes the proud but shows favor to the humble.'"
1 Peter 5:5 NIV

HE'S REALLY BRIGHT

Remember the mission trip to Los Angeles I mentioned at the beginning of this book? While I was joking about the difficulty level of this trip, it was an impactful experience for everyone involved. It was a humbling experience to witness brokenness, poverty, and need so close to home. It reminded us that we don't have to leave our country to reach people; there are people *in our own nation*—even *our own hometowns*—who need Jesus.

One of the most humbling experiences on this trip was hosting a Vacation Bible School event at one of the public parks in Compton. If you know anything about the Los Angeles area, you know that Compton has a high poverty and crime rate. The houses were run down. The yards and public spaces were ravished with weeds and trash. Yet, in the middle of this park, there were happy children whose smiles seemed to brighten up the world around them. I remember thinking that their joy shown brighter because of the lack of happiness around them.

We passed out cookies, coloring sheets, and gifts. We sat with them, played games, and did a few worship songs. At the end of our time together, we listened to a leader from the ministry we partnered with share the gospel with the children in front of an old, desolate baseball field.

Like the yards and parks surrounding it, the stands and baseball field were rundown and abandoned. The fence was falling apart. Although the stands were concrete, they looked so unstable that no one dared to sit or walk up them. The lines of the field were so faint that one could wonder if this field was ever even used to play baseball. And as we were listening to this man preach about Jesus in front of the children, a little boy yelled out, "I see Him!"

We looked at the boy and asked, "Who do you see?"

"Jesus!" He said. His eyes were glistening with joy. "He's sitting in the stands at the baseball field!"

We started looking around, but outside of the children and volunteers, there was no one else in the park or field. We figured he was just making a scene or being silly, but then he said this phrase:

"He's really bright!"

I had read about the glory of the Lord shining in the Bible before,[1] so I wasn't so quick to dismiss this kid's claims anymore.

Although I couldn't see the person he was talking about, who's not to say that this little boy didn't see Jesus?

Now, let's hang on this thought for a minute. Not only did this little boy believe he saw Jesus, which is a miracle in and of itself, but the bigger miracle, in my opinion, is *where* he saw Jesus. He didn't see Jesus in the sanctuary of a 1,000-seat auditorium or strolling the streets of Beverly Hills. Do I believe God's presence is in these places when God's people dwell there? Absolutely! But this kid didn't see Jesus at a church service. He saw Jesus in *Compton. Sitting in a rundown baseball field. In the middle of a Vacation Bible School.*

I'd be lying if this thought didn't cross my mind. I thought, "Why would Jesus be here?" I mean, Jesus is the Son of *God*. He could be anywhere, and yet He was there, in the park, in the heat, amongst the trash on the ground, with us.

As this question roamed through my mind, I heard the Holy Spirit say, "This is *exactly* where Jesus would be if He were here in person." This was the day my perspective changed about Jesus. This was the day I realized the *humility* He displayed and, in return, the humility it takes to be a Christ follower.

Sure, if Jesus was still on earth, He could be anywhere. He could be at churches teaching. He could be at small groups in people's homes. However, if He were here in person, He would be right where that little kid saw Him. He'd be in the messy, broken, dark, lonely, and lost places of the world, bringing hope to those with none. Jesus would choose humility.

That said, we'll be talking about humility in this chapter. As we discuss what humility is, why we need it, and how we get it, I hope you keep this picture of Jesus—*our Jesus*—in your mind. A Jesus that is so bright and glorious and yet, because of humility, can be found in some of the darkest places.

WHAT IS HUMILITY?

"Therefore if you have any encouragement from being united with Christ, if any comfort from His love, if any common sharing in the Spirit, if any tenderness and compassion, then make my joy complete by being like-minded, having the same love, being one in spirit and of one mind. Do nothing out of selfish ambition or vain conceit. Rather, in humility value others above yourselves, not looking to your own interests but each of you to the interests of the others."
2 Philippians 2:1-4 NIV

Humility is a quality we all, as Christians, should desire. In the Sermon on the Mount, one of Jesus's most famous sermons, He shared that the "meek" (or humble) are "blessed," for "they shall inherit the earth."[2] That's a big inheritance! Not only did Jesus *teach* humility, but He also *lived* it. Paul talks of Jesus's humility in Philippians 2:8, saying that He was "found in appearance as a man" and "humbled Himself by becoming obedient to death—even death on a cross!"

Jesus's whole M.O. was humility. Think about it: He was God in human form. *God.* Yet, He decided He'd hunger like us, thirst like us, even—one day, inevitably—die like us. And not only did He die, but He also died a tragic, painful death by one of the most humiliating forms of execution during that time. So, if we're in a pursuit to live like Jesus, then we must pursue humility.

As I've conversed with fellow believers throughout the years, I have found a lot of confusion over what "humility" really is. Is it never speaking up for yourself because that would draw attention? Is it always being the last person to go through the food line? Is it serving behind the scenes instead of being in front of people? Is it never doing anything for yourself and only focusing on others?

According to the Bible, the word "humility" (*tapeinophrosynē* in the original text) means to have "a humble opinion of oneself," "a deep sense of one's littleness," and "modesty, humility, [and] lowliness of mind."[3] In all three of these definitions, I must first point out that humility has everything to do with *you*, which is somewhat ironic since humility also has everything to do with *others*. In other words, humility is self-work that is selfless. It is taking the time to understand ourselves so that we can focus more on others.

The biblical definition of humility begins with our ability to have a "humble opinion" of ourselves by understanding our own "littleness."[4] The Bible speaks to this theme on multiple occasions, but the clearest is in James 4:14, where James writes that we are "mist that appears for a little while and then vanishes." Have you ever seen mist or fog? When I was little, I, like all children, had trouble pronouncing words now and then. I, for some reason, could not bring myself to say the word "foggy" when there was a morning mist. Instead, I ran to my mom and told her it was "froggy" outside. So, inevitably, when I think about mist, I think about frogs.

But seriously, if you've ever witnessed fog or mist, you know that, especially as you're driving, it gets really thick suddenly, and then it's gone. It consumes your vision for a few seconds, and then it's nothing more than haze in your rearview mirror.

James is telling us in James 4 that our lives are like fog! It consumes our vision, desires, and time, but in an instance, it's *gone*, never to return. While this may be a more profound and darker concept for us to grasp, our understanding of our eternal littleness is necessary to pursue humility. We must understand that, as humans, there are limitations. No matter how wonderful or powerful a person can be, he or she will never live forever. Some boundaries have been set for us. We cannot hold our breath forever. We cannot breathe underwater naturally. We cannot survive without water and food. Half of us can't even seem to survive a one-hour social media crash that forces us to talk to people in real life!

When we think about our natural limitations and the fact that our lives are also limited, we understand our own littleness. But how can we know if something is little unless it is compared to something big? Our understanding of our littleness can only come from understanding God's greatness. God is not subject to boundaries or limitations; He does not need sleep, food, or breath. Now don't get me wrong—God is always true to His character and will faithfully uphold His Name. He will not act out of the boundaries He set for Himself, but here's the crucial thing to remember: 1) God created the boundaries, and 2) God can change the boundaries if He wants.

God is not subject to limitations, but guess what? He chose limits when He chose to send Jesus to the earth. Jesus was entirely God and fully human, which means He had all the power of God the Father with all the puny, little limitations of a human. His words carried the power to raise people from the dead, but we also read in the Bible that Jesus had to take naps.[5] A touch of His hand could heal someone from disease, but Jesus also had to eat and drink to stay healthy. Demons obeyed every word from Jesus, but He also had a career as a carpenter to support His ministry.[6] Why? Because of these limitations, Jesus was humbled. Jesus was the ultimate example of humility because He was subject to humanity, and now we pursue humility because it's a part of who Jesus is.

Before we move on, I want to point out another definition of humility that will clarify a few things. At this moment, you probably have a deep sense of your own littleness. You probably feel convicted about a few things. You probably feel an urgency to make the most of your life since your time is limited. And while all of those are good things to feel, as Pastor Rick Warren put it,

"Humility is not thinking less of yourself; it is thinking of yourself less."[7]

It's possible to know your littleness while also being confident in your gifting, calling, and anointing. The key to humility is that you're self-aware but choose to focus on others. You understand your littleness, but you also understand that God has called you and chosen you "for such a time as this."[8] You know your worth, value, calling, and gifting. Still, you choose to use that worth, value, calling, and gifting to serve others. Humility is all about you, but it's also all about others.

WHY DO I NEED HUMILITY?

"Humility is the fear of the LORD; its wages are riches and honor and life."
Proverbs 22:4 NIV

Humility is not "sexy." As one author put it, "humility was no more valued in [the Apostle] Paul's day than it is in our day. Both worlds were, and are, populated by prideful people."[9] Humility, unfortunately, is not what Hollywood classifies as one of the "top 10 qualities" of a successful person. Outside of the church, humility may as well be weakness to a world that thrives on pride, self-focus, and vain conceit. However, to God, humility is attractive, which is why we need to pursue it.

Proverbs 22:4 says, "Humility is the fear of the Lord; its wages are riches and honor and life." In other words, God gives riches, honor, and life to those who are humble. Doesn't that sound amazing? And doesn't that sound contradictory to what the world teaches us? The world says to make it all about "you," work harder than everyone else, and beat everyone else out to be the richest person alive. However, God's Word tells us that the way to riches is not through vain conceit or selfish ambition but *humility*. In addition to this list of blessings we find in Proverbs 22:4, the Bible has more to say about the effects of humility. Here are a few more benefits in the Bible that come from pursuing humility:

- Being exalted by God (James 4:10 and Luke 14:11)
- God's ear, His forgiveness, and His healing (2 Chronicles 7:14)
- Favor (Proverbs 3:34)
- Wisdom (Proverbs 11:2)
- Guidance and knowledge (Psalm 25:9)
- Victory (Psalm 149:4)
- God's strength (2 Corinthians 12:9)
- Delight (2 Corinthians 12:10)

Who wouldn't want all these things? Every one of these verses referenced above could have been our theme verse for this section. However, I chose to discuss Proverbs 22:4 because it specifically references the "fear of the Lord," and we can't talk about humility without discussing the fear of the Lord.

First, let's discuss what this "fear of the Lord" thing is. When you read the words "fear" and "Lord" in the same sentence, you probably had one of these thoughts:

"I thought God was love. Why should I fear Him?"
"I thought God was kind. Why should I be afraid?"
"How can I fear God if I'm supposed to love Him?"

These are all reasonable questions to be asking yourself right now. I understand because I asked them, too. The word "fear" can mean being scared or terrified of something. However, in this context, it uses the original word *yir'â*, which means "respect, reverence, [or] piety."[10]

Think about the Proverbs 22:4 kind of fear like this. When you were a little kid and did something that you knew your parents would be upset about, you were probably afraid. Maybe you were afraid of getting a spanking. Perhaps you were afraid of being sent to your room. Even so, chances are you were also scared because you didn't want to disappoint your parents. You didn't want to go through telling them what happened and seeing their reaction. You didn't want them to give you consequences. And whether you knew it then or not, that fear came from the respect you had for your parents. You were afraid of them because you honored them.

Similarly, this is how we should view fear of the Lord—not necessarily as fear of telling Him what we've done or being afraid of getting punished, but as overwhelming respect and awe of who He is that makes us want to be the best we can be and do the best we can do to obey Him. Proverbs 22:4 says, "Humility *is* the fear of the Lord" (emphasis mine). This means that without fearing God, it's impossible to be humble. Why? Because being humble means honoring God, not ourselves. Fear of the Lord is the beginning of every blessing, including all the benefits listed in Proverbs 22:4! I'll prove it to you with this diagram:

Fear of the Lord → humility → obedience → blessing

We begin by fearing the Lord, honoring Him, and worshiping Him as the King of Kings and Lord of Lords. Then, we are humbled by His awesomeness. We are humbled that a God like that would choose people like us. Then, from a place of humility, we have no choice but to obey because how could we disobey someone so great and powerful? We *want* to obey because we know He has good things in store! Finally, we receive our blessing—riches, honor, and life—along with the other benefits mentioned at this section's beginning.

So, why do we pursue humility? Because without humility, it is impossible to receive God's blessing. James 4:6 says that God "opposes the proud but shows favor to the humble." You must pursue humility if you want blessings from God and His grace and favor. God cannot bless pride, a deep pleasure or satisfaction derived from our achievements. Look at James 4:6 again. It says that God *opposes* the proud. I don't know about you, but I don't want to be in opposition to God! I would not win.

We know what humility is. We understand that we need it to receive blessings from God. Now, let's discuss how we get humility because, if you've ever struggled with pride (aka all of us), it's easier said than done—but not impossible.

HOW DO I GET HUMILITY?

"In the same way, you who are younger, submit yourselves to your elders. All of you, clothe yourselves with humility toward one another, because, 'God opposes the proud but shows favor to the humble.'"
1 Peter 5:5 NIV

We've discussed what humility is and why we need it, so now we get to do the practical work of learning how to pursue humility every day. In short, the way to get humility is to submit. I know that many women reading this book may *hate* that word. I understand. I used to hate it, too. I thought it was so unfair that, as women, we were expected to "submit" to anyone and anything. However, that was a poor connotation of Scripture and teaching, and on behalf of whoever told you something about submission that's made you resist it with every bone in your body, I apologize. To move forward in pursuing humility daily, we must have a positive (and biblical) understanding of submission, so let's break it down.

In our theme verse for this section, 1 Peter 5:5, the word "submit" is the word *hypotassō* in the original Greek. *Hypotassō* means to "arrange under," to "subject oneself," to "obey," and to "yield to one's admonition or advice."[11] Depending on your upbringing, those words may have made you a little defensive. However, I want you to see that submission is a helpful act that has the components of choice, love, and security.

Submission is something that we must choose. It is a choice we make as individuals to "arrange under; to subject oneself; to obey; to yield to one's admonition or advice." We decide who we submit to. Period.

Biblical submission responds out of love, not hatred or fear. Paul clarifies that a woman will only submit to her husband *if her husband loves her.*[12] Paul also implies that husbands will have difficulty loving their wives *if they refuse to submit.*[13] It's a cycle and system that God created for marriage. If there's no love, it's difficult to submit. If there's no submission, it's difficult to love.

Lastly, submission results in security. Whether it's a love relationship, work relationship, or spiritual relationship, safety comes through submission. As a wife, I feel the most secure—not just because I have a hunk of a husband that can physically protect me, but because I know that multiple layers of submission cover me. I'm submitted to my husband. My husband is submitted to leadership and God. His leadership is also submitted to other people and God. At least five layers of submission cover me. That's a really soft cushion, people!

These layers of protection mean that when I must make a decision or choose a path, I have layers of covering from humble people, which means I have layers and layers of people who are blessed because God shows favor to the humble.[14] If I want God's blessing, what better way to receive it than to be advised by those who have already received it?

Everything we discussed about submission is true for our relationship with the Lord and with people. When it comes to submitting, there is choice, love, and security intertwined. Now that we have a better biblical understanding of submission, let's discuss how submission can help us pursue humility daily.

We understand that submission is a needed part of pursuing humility, but who exactly do we submit ourselves to? Everyone? Only some people? Only "real" Christians? Only God? To answer that question, let's look at three categories of who we should submit to. By submitting in these areas, we are actively choosing to pursue humility every day.

Submit to Christ.

First and foremost, we must submit to Christ and let Him run our lives. Ephesians 5:24 says wives should submit to their husbands "as the church submits to Christ." And just so you know, the "church" in this sentence does not mean the place you go to every Sunday. The "church" means the global community of believers. That means that if you're a believer, you *are* the church. And as the church, you are called to submit to Christ, adhere to His advice, and yield to His truth. As we submit to Jesus, we pursue humility in our relationship with Him.

Submit to Covering.

The second area we submit to is covering. As 1 Peter 5:5 says, we must submit ourselves to our "elders." In reality, these "elders" can be anyone in our lives that looks out for us and our well-being. Our covering could be our pastors, parents, spouse, teacher, boss—you name it. Elders are people who have either been put in leadership over us by position or by our choice. Either way, Romans 13:1 says that "the authorities that exist have been established by God." Therefore, we should "submit" ourselves to them.[15] Even if our boss is "evil" or our parents "totally don't understand us," those authorities have still been established by God. While we should never obey an instruction contradictory to God's Word, we should always honor those in authority by submitting to our covering.

Submit to Community.

Lastly, we are to submit to community. This point may be one of my favorite points in this book! In addition to submitting ourselves to the elders, 1 Peter 5:5 says that we should "clothe ourselves with humility toward one another." This section of the verse means that we are to arrange ourselves under others as well. "Community" in this point means our peers, classmates, teammates, co-workers, acquaintances, brothers and sisters in Christ, etc.

Community is a catch-all for every person we're around. Does "submitting" to community mean that we do everything people tell us to do? No. What it means is that we honor them, recognize their importance, and choose to take the lower seat. Jesus is our example when it comes to submitting to community. The Bible says in Philippians 2:5 that we are to "have the same mindset as Christ Jesus" in "our relationships with one another." It then spends the following few verses talking about Jesus's humility and submission, ultimately to death.[16]

As we choose to submit to Christ, covering, and community, we will be well on our way to pursuing humility daily!

Daily Declaration

"I believe humility is God's desire for me. I choose to live a life that gives God the glory instead of giving myself the glory for accomplishments, relationships, and opportunities. I will joyfully submit to Christ, my covering, and my community. As I submit to these areas, I believe God will bless my humble heart. I choose to fear the Lord above everything and everyone else, and I choose to praise Him for every good thing that happens in my life."

8

PURSUE FORGIVENESS

"Then Peter came to Jesus and asked, 'Lord, how many times shall I forgive my brother or sister who sins against me? Up to seven times?' Jesus answered, 'I tell you, not seven times, but seventy-seven times.'"
Matthew 18:21-22 NIV

SUPER NINTENDO NIGHTS

The story I'm about to tell has been told to me because, let's face it, at two months old, I couldn't remember a thing.

It was Christmas morning after our family had opened all the presents. My older brother, Seth, and my dad had gotten a new Super Nintendo game—Donkey Kong. This is the same game that I grew up playing with Seth and my dad on our Super Nintendo. Yes, we still have it. And yes, it's still the most fun thing to play.

On that Christmas morning, my brother and dad were playing Super Nintendo. Mom was sitting in a chair somewhere in our living room. I was lying down, being a two-month-old baby on a blanket on our living room floor. I was lying there doing what babies do best—absolutely nothing. And as my dad and Seth played their video game, something happened. Maybe Donkey Kong missed a banana. Maybe they lost and only had one balloon left. I'm not sure what event prompted this response, but my dad, at the top of his lungs, yelled, "NO!"

As I said, I can't remember this event, but I know that my dad is one of the sweetest men alive and rarely raises his voice. So, as you can imagine, baby Emily was shocked when her dad yelled. And as the story goes, I wouldn't look at my father for the rest of the day. *Not even a glance.*

Somehow, my little baby mind had associated his screaming at the game with him yelling at me, and my little baby feelings were hurt. Therefore, I refused to be around him because I was offended.

Now, the truth is, I could have put a lot of stories here. I've only lived 25 years at this point, but I've lived long enough to experience some offense and hurt. There have been plenty of times when I didn't want to look at, be around, or talk to someone for the day—or more! And I bet you can probably relate unless you're like a *perfect person*. Maybe it's not being yelled at or loud noises, but I can bet there's something in your life that has caused you to feel offended. It could be getting cut off in traffic. It could be an offense like receiving a bad grade on a test or not receiving an invite to a birthday party. It could be a random slight or feeling of rejection from someone you loved.

Regardless of what it is for you, we've all been hurt at some point, which means that we've all been in situations that require forgiveness, and forgiveness can be *hard*. However, even though it can be challenging, forgiveness is always possible.

What does the Bible say about forgiveness? Why is it essential to our walk with God? How do we get to a place where we can forgive those who have hurt us? Let's discuss it together.

WHAT IS FORGIVENESS?

"Then Peter came to Jesus and asked, 'Lord, how many times shall I forgive my brother or sister who sins against me? Up to seven times?' Jesus answered, 'I tell you, not seven times, but seventy-seven times.'"
Matthew 18:21-22 NIV

The word "forgive" used in the verse above and various times throughout the New Testament comes from the Greek word *aphiēmi*. *Aphiēmi* is one word that encompasses three actions: to let go, to let alone, and to let be.[1] In English, to describe the process of letting go, letting alone, and letting be, we use the single word "forgive" in the Bible. However, if you were to look up the definition of "forgive" right now, you would find a definition that looks like this:

To forgive means to stop feeling angry or resentful toward [someone] for an offense, flaw, or mistake.[2]

I'll be honest. I think the dictionary writers tried their best to define forgiveness. It's a complicated word and an even more complicated action. Even so, I must point out a flaw in this terminology. In the dictionary definition, the act of forgiveness is related to *feeling*. The definition tells us to stop "feeling" angry or resentful toward someone to achieve true forgiveness. It doesn't say anything about the forgiveness process or what healthy forgiveness looks like. According to the worldly definition, forgiveness happens when your "ugly" feelings subside.

However, looking at the biblical definition of forgiveness, *aphiēmi*, you will see that there is nothing about feeling involved. In fact, the definition of *aphiēmi* is strictly action. Understanding the difference between the two definitions is crucial in pursuing forgiveness. You have to know the correct definition because if you do not know what you're pursuing, chances are, you will never reach it. If you are judging your ability to forgive someone by the way you *feel*, you'll never know if you've actually forgiven that person. A recent study found that there are 27 emotions that "blend together in our everyday experience[s]" to produce our feelings.[3] What this tells me (and scientists) is that our emotions cannot be trusted. They intertwine and react to each other to form a concoction of diverse and ever-changing feelings. Therefore, if your whole goal with forgiveness is to stop "feeling" a certain way, good luck. When you forgive someone simply to change the way you feel, 1) it's highly unlikely to work and 2) that's only focusing on *you*. There is no part of forgiveness in that system that has to do with anyone or anything else.

However, if you judge your ability to forgive by the way you *live*, you'll know right away if you've actually forgiven someone. And I'll prove it to you.

Say that you're in a fight with a close friend. Your friend sent a text to your phone saying something wrong about you that was meant to be sent to another person. You read the text, and you're heartbroken. How could your friend think about you like that? How could she talk about you like that? Tensions rise, and now you and your friend are no longer speaking. You feel betrayed, forgotten, embarrassed, and angry. Each day, you pray for God to take away those feelings. "Once I stop feeling this way, I'll forgive her," you think. "Or maybe when these feelings go away, I'll know

I am over this and have fully forgiven her." But day after day, the feelings remain the same, so you assume that forgiveness is impossible, and that friendship is ruined. You keep avoiding your friend and read the text message she sent you repeatedly. You think, "I want to forgive, but I'm too hurt," and whether you realize it or not, you choose to let your feelings dictate how you live. And because you are unable to truly forgive, you are unable to truly live.

I don't think there's anything wrong with asking God to help you forgive someone or take away emotions you don't want to feel. However, there is *so much more* than feeling involved when it comes to forgiveness! Emotions are indicators that signify something is going on in our hearts. When we pray for our feelings to subside, we're really praying for God to fix the symptom, not the disease. When our goal is to get rid of "ugly" emotions—which, by the way, don't exist—we're actually doing ourselves a disservice. We're asking God to treat the symptom of a disease when He could very well cure the cause. This idea of shallow forgiveness is why I can't get on board with the dictionary definition.

However, I absolutely, 100% can get on board with the biblical version of forgiveness. I can support and pursue *aphiēmi* all day long. Why? Because it's God's way of forgiveness. Sure, there are feelings involved, but there is also action. The emotions that we feel point to actions that we must take, and God's way of forgiving gives us a perfect game plan for the process to forgive.

So, throughout this chapter, as we're discussing forgiveness, here's what we mean:

Let go.

If an offense, flaw, hardship, or pain has occurred in your life, the first step to forgiveness is to let it go. Letting it go does not mean that you forget what happened or try to play it down; to let go means recognizing the offense's magnitude yet still choosing to release it. Picture the hand of someone who has hurt you in your hand. Then picture letting go of the hand and watching the person fade in the distance. It doesn't make the person or hurt any less real; it just makes the person separate from you.

Let alone.

Once you let it go, it's time to let it alone. Letting alone means that you don't continue to go back to the offense or hurt and try to dig it up. Forgiveness does not mean reconciliation. Forgiveness is a one-way street between you and the Lord. Once it's done, *it's done*. Once it's gone, *it's gone*. Don't be a friend to your pain. Let it alone. Just like when you unplug a lamp from the wall and the light turns off, if you take away the source of energy, power, and life from an offense, it will disintegrate.

Let be.

Forgiveness also means to let it be. Have you ever heard that Beatles song? "Let it be, let it be, let it be, let it be. Speaking words of wisdom, let it be."[4] The Beatles said it best: *There is wisdom in letting something be.* To "let be" means not only to let it go or let it alone but also to let it have the freedom to run its course. Letting an offense or person "be" means letting them live their lives and not being captivated or caught up in what's happening. It is not our job to keep tabs or cause trouble on someone who has hurt us. Romans 12:19 makes it clear that God is the one who will avenge wrongdoing, not you.[5] So let it be.

This is the biblical definition of true forgiveness: **to let go, let alone**, and **let be**. It's not about feelings. It's not about revenge. It's not about forgetting. It's about taking action to move past the offense so you can live the life God has always intended for you. This forgiveness is the forgiveness that we must pursue daily.

WHY SHOULD I FORGIVE?
"Be kind and compassionate to one another, forgiving each other, just as in Christ God forgave you."
Ephesians 4:32 NIV

Why can't we hold grudges, be "bitter" and "salty," and mind our own business? Why can't we never trust or love people again? Why can't we play it safe and not open our hearts?

The answer is simple, and it's found in Ephesians 4:23. We must pursue forgiveness because God forgave us.[6]

One of my all-time favorite quotes is from one of my former pastors. During a Sunday message, he talked about how he responds when people ask his opinion on hot topics. "What's your opinion on President so-and-so?" or "What's your opinion on this-and-that?"

His response went along the lines of this: "I don't have an opinion. When I became a Christian, I gave up my right to an opinion. If you want to know my opinion, it's in the Bible."

Boom.

Do you ever really need another answer to complex questions after hearing that? My pastor made it clear that his thoughts and feelings were not as important as God's thoughts and feelings, which we can see in His Word. The Bible says that when we become Christians, we are "crucified with Christ," and it is "no longer [we] who live, but Christ lives in [us]."[7] Therefore, the opinions, thoughts, preferences, etc. we had before we met Christ no longer have a place. When we become Christ followers, we adopt Christ's mindset, lifestyle, preferences, and thoughts.

What does all of this have to do with forgiveness? Well, if you believe that you have a reason to harbor unforgiveness or hold an offense over someone's head, then that means you're listening to your own opinion. We are called to forgive others as believers in Jesus because we have accepted His forgiveness. If you've *received* forgiveness, then you're obligated to *give* forgiveness.

Think of it this way. If I hadn't eaten in three days and was starving, and someone gave me 24/7 access to a fully stocked buffet, I'd consider myself blessed. I could eat, be full, and never worry about going hungry again. There's more food at this buffet than I will ever need in my life! Then, one day, a person comes up to me and asks if I have any food to give. They say they haven't eaten in ten days, and if I don't provide them with food, they will die. And I, with my fully stocked, 24/7 buffet, say, "Yes, I do have food. I have an *overabundance* of it, actually. More than I will ever need for myself. But you can't have any."

What?

This analogy may be dramatic, but this is what happens when we choose not to forgive someone. The Bible says that we were "dead in [our] transgressions and sins,"[8] and then Jesus came along and saved us. He forgave us of our wrongdoings—past, present, and future. Therefore, we have more forgiveness available to us than we will ever need! There will never be a scenario where we can out-sin God's forgiveness (unless we blaspheme the Holy Spirit,[9] but that's a topic for another day).

God has forgiven us more than we could ever need through His Son Jesus, and because we have been so freely forgiven, God asks us to share His forgiveness with others. Just as it is with everything in God's Kingdom, forgiveness is not just for you. Forgiveness equips you to forgive others.

Now, to those of you who are still having a hard time forgiving those who have hurt you, I get it. I don't want it to sound like I'm getting onto you or making fun of you for struggling with unforgiveness. I understand what it's like to be violated, sinned against, and hurt. I understand what it's like not to want to forgive someone. I understand that you think holding onto unforgiveness gives you a hold on the person who hurt you. I understand that having this hold makes you feel like you're in control, which means you can now control the hurt.

But may I help you for a moment? Do you realize that when you're holding onto unforgiveness, it's actually causing *you* more harm than *them*? As much as we'd like to picture the perpetrator sitting at home crying and mourning over what they've done to us and how they wish we'd let them back into our lives, chances are, they're not thinking about us *at all*. That may be harsh, but it's the truth, and the Bible says that the "truth will set you free."[10] Accepting the truth that unforgiveness is hurting you more than who you're trying to hurt will set you FREE. And I know you want to be free because you've read this far.

Does this mean the offender will get off home free with no consequences? Absolutely not. God's Word makes it very clear that He will avenge you:

- "Do not take revenge, my dear friends, but leave room for God's wrath, for it is written: 'It is mine to avenge; I will repay,' says the Lord." (Romans 12:19)
- "Do not say, 'I'll pay you back for this wrong!' Wait for the Lord, and He will avenge you." (Proverbs 20:22)
- "For we know Him who said, 'It is mine to avenge; I will repay,' and again, 'The Lord will judge His people.'" (Hebrews 10:30)

Because we, as Christians, have been forgiven by Christ, we must forgive others. We can't hold onto our unforgiveness because God has given us an abundance of forgiveness.

Forgiveness can be challenging, unnatural, and sometimes even painful. Still, if you're a believer in Jesus, true forgiveness is available today, and it's available to you because you've already received it.

HOW DO I PURSUE FORGIVENESS?
"But I tell you, love your enemies and pray for those who persecute you."
Matthew 5:44 NIV

As we've learned throughout this chapter, pursuing forgiveness daily is a choice against our natural tendencies. However, this is a choice that can be made when we choose to forgive God's way.

Matthew 5:44 gives us an outline of God's plan for forgiveness, and it's everything but ordinary. During Jesus's famous Sermon on the Mount, He tells the crowd to "love [their] enemies and pray for those who persecute" them."[11]

Hold up. We're supposed to *love* the people that are our enemies? And *pray* for the people that persecute us? What kind of plan is this?

God's plan.

And praise God it is because if it weren't, *He wouldn't have forgiven us.* Jesus represented this plan for forgiveness perfectly on the cross. God sent Jesus to the earth out of love.[12] As Jesus was being crucified, He prayed, "Father, forgive them, for they do not know what they are doing."[13] Jesus prayed for the people who were crucifying Him, and interestingly, He was praying for God to forgive them.

God calls us to love our enemies and pray for those who hurt us. This system is the way to forgive them truly, but here's the kicker: You can't forgive someone if you're not praying for them, and you can't pray for someone if you don't love them.

What does that mean? It means that to pray for someone and forgive them, you must love them first. The word "love" used in Matthew 5:44 is *agapaō*, God's love. We talked about this in chapter 4! Knowing the specific kind of love God is asking us to operate from in the forgiveness process is essential. If we tried to love our enemies out of our earthly love, it wouldn't work (27 competing emotions, remember?). I don't know about you, but my human capacity to love someone who has hurt me is very slim!

However, there is no limit when we love those who have hurt us with *agapaō*. There's an infinite capacity. God's love lasts *forever*,[14] which means it's more than enough to forgive an offense. 1 Peter 4:8 says that "love covers over a multitude of sins." How much sin is a "multitude"? I'm not sure, but I can guarantee it's more than just two or three. And yet the Bible says that love covers them all.

So, how do we forgive others? How do we pursue forgiveness daily? How do we forgive God's way? We love people with the love of God, and we pray for those who have hurt us.

Loving others with the love of God means that we understand that no matter how difficult it may be for us, God still loves the people who have hurt us. God still cares about them. God still has a plan for their lives, and ultimately, His plan for forgiveness still prevails. God's command in Mark 12:31 to "love [our] neighbors as [ourselves]" still stands. When we love those who have hurt us with *agapaō*, God's love, we choose to forgive them because we know that God loves them.

Proverbs 17:9 says, "Love prospers when a fault is forgiven, but dwelling on it separates close friends." Let love prosper as you forgive those who have hurt you, and let love prosper by praying for them.

Prayer is love expressed. And let me just clarify this: Prayers of forgiveness aren't praying for the person to be hit with karma or a bus. No, this prayer is praying for them to be well, blessed, and ultimately know the love of God. As we love people, our desire to pray for them will grow, and as we pray for people, our love for them will grow.

Daily Declaration

"I believe that I am free from unforgiveness. Right now, I choose to forgive those who have hurt me. Even if my feelings don't change, I know that forgiveness has taken place. I choose to forgive freely because I have been forgiven freely by God. I will not hoard His forgiveness but graciously give it to everyone around me. Ultimately, I trust God and know that if anyone sins against me, it is His offense to avenge, not mine. I choose to pray for and love those who have hurt me, and I choose to live in forgiveness every day."

9

PURSUE AWARENESS

"Anyone you forgive, I also forgive. And what I have forgiven—if there was anything to forgive—I have forgiven in the sight of Christ for your sake, in order that Satan might not outwit us. For we are not unaware of his schemes."
2 Corinthians 2:10-11 NIV

NOT A COINCIDENCE

"This is it," I thought. "This is the moment I've been waiting for."

I had just received a text from our executive pastor asking me to join a panel for our church's women's night a few weeks away. We would answer questions from the stage the attendees submitted through their registration forms, and I was so excited to be a part. It'd been nearly three years since I'd had a chance to share from a platform, and I was looking forward to the opportunity.

In the weeks leading up to the women's event, I was more excited than nervous. Anytime I have a chance to speak publicly, there are some nerves, not necessarily from fear or anxiety but from the weight and responsibility of sharing God's Word with people. I talked to my husband about it almost daily, and we were both praying for the event and what would be shared. I didn't know the topic I'd be speaking about yet, and I only had five minutes, but I was determined to make those five minutes matter.

A few days before the event, I became anxious. My heart rate increased. I started shaking. My mind was going 100 miles a minute. I had dealt with anxiety and stress in the past here and there but *never* to this degree. "This is insane!" I thought. "I'm not an anxious person!" I found myself trapped in a feeling of anxiousness, wishing that the excitement would come back. Instead of looking forward to the women's night, I began to dread it out of fear that something would go wrong.

I began to express my worries and fears to Austin, and, as the incredible husband that he is, he graciously reminded me of the importance of *awareness*. Now, Austin and I have been in ministry long enough to know that it's not a coincidence when things like the anxiety I felt happen close to significant events. And it was no coincidence that the day before the event, I got a text from our executive pastor saying that my topic to discuss on women's night was *anxiety*.

Wow. Shocker.

It's no coincidence that I hadn't had an anxiety attack in years, and yet, the moment before I'm supposed to share about it, it hits once again. However, the best part about being aware of the enemy's schemes is that we know that God will use all of them for good.[1] While the enemy meant for the anxiety I felt to keep me from sharing with other women, it actually added fuel to the fire. It made what I had to say more impactful. I wasn't sharing about anxiety from a stand-offish approach; I was sharing about anxiety and God's mighty hand *right from the middle of it.*

The thing about awareness is that, without it, we are completely oblivious and helpless. I once had someone tell me, "If you don't see it, you're not responsible for it. But once you see it, it's your responsibility." How can I be held accountable for something unless I know what it is? How can I take responsibility for a problem or action unless someone points it out to me?

Just like the light bulb went off for Austin and me when we found out my topic for the women's night, that "ah-ha!" moment where everything made sense, I believe there are things God wants to reveal to us to make us more aware. I think there are things in our hearts and minds that God wants to uncover. I believe there's an awareness of the enemy and his schemes that we need to understand. Therefore, this chapter is devoted to pursuing awareness daily. If we pursue awareness, we will see and understand things we didn't see or understand before. And through this insight and understanding, we can take responsibility and stand firm against the enemy and his schemes, knowing that God is ultimately using it for our good.

WHAT IS AWARENESS?

"Anyone you forgive, I also forgive. And what I have forgiven—if there was anything to forgive—I have forgiven in the sight of Christ for your sake, in order that Satan might not outwit us. For we are not unaware of his schemes."
2 Corinthians 2:10-11 NIV

Have you ever been in a situation where you were completely unaware of what was going on around you? We see it in the media, social platforms, memes, etc. We see the videos of newscasters reading their scripts and, in the background, someone does something crazy. We see pictures and memes of people taking family photos, and in the background, there's something wild happening. Maybe we're in a store, waiting in line, and a discussion is happening right behind us, and we have no idea. Perhaps we're out for a walk, and suddenly it starts to rain. Regardless of what scenario you may have found yourself in, we can all agree that there have been moments in our lives where we've been unaware of a situation.

Our theme verse for this chapter is found in 2 Corinthians 2. This verse discusses the importance of being aware of the enemy's (Satan's) schemes. As believers in Jesus Christ, we must develop an awareness of these schemes. The word "unaware" in 2 Corinthians 2:11 means "to be ignorant, not to know; not to understand, unknown."[2] To be unaware of something means to not only miss it but also to misunderstand it entirely. Therefore, the awareness that we're pursuing is more than knowing *what* is happening. It's understanding *why* it's happening.

The What

As I hope you know by now, we, as Christians, have an enemy, and his name is Satan. While our God is beautiful, kind, considerate, mighty, and all-powerful, Satan is ugly, mean, selfish, weak, and jealous. Even though there is no comparison in the amount of power Satan has compared to God's power, the Bible makes it clear that Satan does have some power, and with that power, he has set out to accomplish specific plans—plans that involve *you*. 2 Corinthians 2:10-11 urges us as believers to be aware of these plans so that when they occur, we will be prepared to respond correctly. Here's what the Bible has to say about these "schemes" of the enemy:

- He's constantly seeking people to devour (1 Peter 5:8)
- He can disguise himself as something good (2 Corinthians 11:14)
- He comes only to steal, kill, and destroy (John 10:10)

- He's a murderer and a liar (John 8:44)
- He's a deceiver (Revelation 12:9)
- He blinds the eyes of unbelievers so they can't see clearly (2 Corinthians 4:4)
- He works through disobedience (Ephesians 2:2)
- He is the ruler of *this* world (John 14:30, John 12:31, 2 Corinthians 4:3-4)
- He's an accuser (Revelation 12:10)
- He works through a spirit of fear (2 Timothy 1:7)
- He's crafty (Genesis 3:1)
- He employs demonic spirits (Revelation 16:14)
- He's cursed (Matthew 25:41)
- He has his own will (2 Timothy 2:26)
- He will make you question God's Word (Genesis 3:1-6)
- He's an oppressor (Acts 10:38)
- He's a tempter (1 Thessalonians 3:5)
- He's the angel of the bottomless pit (Revelation 9:11)

As you can see from this list, the enemy's schemes are anything but few and far between. There are many plans, tactics, and identities that the enemy can deploy to take us away from our pursuit of Jesus. However, as believers in Jesus, we have the victory! Philippians 2:10-11 says, "At the name of Jesus every knee should bow, in heaven and on earth and under the earth, and every tongue will acknowledge that Jesus Christ is Lord, to the glory of God the Father."

Remember how we said that Satan was the god of *this* world? That means he's included in those who will bow before Jesus and acknowledge He is Lord, both on and under the earth! So, don't fear the enemy's schemes or tactics. However, be aware that you have an enemy who does not want you to succeed, and don't be surprised when his schemes seemingly try to creep into your life.

The Why

Why is Satan set on destroying us? Well, here's the deal. Satan isn't set on destroying us just because he feels like it. At the end of the day, we're not the target at all. Satan targets us to get to the heart of God.

Let's face it—Satan doesn't have any beef with us. He has a lot of beef with God. And since the "Spirit of Him who raised Jesus from the dead is living in [us],"[3] the enemy wants us destroyed. Do you remember how Jesus's blood on the cross made our sins "white as snow,"[4] and since the blood of Jesus covers us, that's all God sees when He looks at us? Well, the same is true for Satan. He couldn't honestly care less about you because when he sees you, he sees Jesus.

But why all the hatred and rage? Why is there so much animosity? Why is Satan determined to destroy us because we are God's children? There are multiple answers to these questions, and they all stem from pride.

The Bible makes it clear that at one point, Satan was in heaven.[5] In fact, he was one of the most beautiful angels! But because of pride, he fell from heaven. He wanted the worship and glory to be his instead of reflecting it to God,[6] so he got kicked out of heaven. And since he's been kicked out of the presence of God, he wants us to be away from God's presence as well. *He* wants to be worshiped and in charge. He wants people to follow *him*. And ultimately, he wants people to *disobey God*.

All of Satan's schemes are set on removing us from God's presence—for *eternity*. But thank God for the salvation of Jesus that offers eternal hope! When we are saved, we spend eternity with God. We no longer worry about separation from God or spending eternity in hell. However, while Satan can never remove you from God's presence, he can cause you to question the value and validity of God's presence through sin. Being saved does not make us exempt from the attacks of the enemy or temptation of sin, and therefore, we must pursue awareness.

WHY DO I NEED TO BE AWARE?

"This is what the Lord says to you: 'Do not be afraid or discouraged because of this vast army. For the battle is not yours, but God's."
2 Chronicles 20:15 NIV

2 Chronicles 20 tells the story of King Jehoshaphat defeating Moab and Ammon, two nations battling against Israel. As the Moabite and Ammonite armies approached, the people of Israel were terrified. "There's no way we can beat them!" they thought. But as King Jehoshaphat began to pray, God spoke to him through a prophet and passed along an important message:

"Listen, King Jehoshaphat and all who live in Judah and Jerusalem! This is what the Lord says to you: 'Do not be afraid or discouraged because of this vast army. For the battle is not yours, but God's. Tomorrow march down against them. They will be climbing up by the Pass of Ziz, and you will find them at the end of the gorge in the Desert of Jeruel. You will not have to fight this battle. Take up your positions; stand firm and see the deliverance the Lord will give you, Judah and Jerusalem. Do not be afraid; do not be discouraged. Go out to face them tomorrow, and the Lord will be with you.'" - *2 Chronicles 20:15-17 NIV*

There are a few things I would like to point out from these verses that I believe answer the question "why?" when it comes to being aware of Satan's schemes. In 2 Chronicles 20, we see the

Israelite army engaged in an actual war, but I believe that these verses set the stage for how we, as Christians, are to fight spiritual wars. We may not all find ourselves on a battlefield fighting in the physical realm, but according to the Bible, we will all find ourselves on the battlefield fighting in the spiritual realm. We will discuss spiritual warfare and what it means to "fight" the enemy later in this chapter, but for now, let's continue with our discussion of 2 Chronicles 20.

First, God tells King Jehoshaphat and all the Israelites to not be afraid or discouraged. We must pursue awareness because, without it, we will find ourselves afraid and discouraged without hope. When it comes to spiritual warfare, I believe one of the enemy's greatest tactics is to get Christians to forfeit abundant life in Jesus by being unwilling to engage in the fight. So often we see people wave the white flag and surrender—not to God's will, but to the plan of the enemy. A few months ago, I prayed for someone who said they were experiencing spiritual attacks like crazy. She noticed that these attacks had heightened after she had the opportunity to do her dream job, something she believed God was calling her to do (again, no coincidences). As we talked, she expressed to me that she was strongly considering not taking the job opportunity in hopes that the attacks would cease.

In that moment, I'll admit I was angry. I wasn't angry at the woman who had asked for prayer. I was angry at the enemy who had somehow convinced this lady that living outside of her purpose *without* spiritual attacks was better than living within God's perfect will *with* spiritual attacks. She had allowed fear and discouragement from the battle she was facing to keep her from the blessing God had for her.

One of the greatest revelations I have ever received from the Lord is that fear is simply an attack on focus. Think about it. When you're overwhelmingly afraid of something, it is all you can think about. You're not thinking about positive outcomes or resting on God's Word. When you're afraid, all you can focus on is the thing that's causing your fear!

Before the Israelites even went to battle, God reassured them to not be afraid or discouraged. He told them that they would be facing a vast army, which means the threat they were facing was significant. He wasn't downplaying the enemy force or the fear they would feel when they showed up to fight. However, He comforted them with these words as they became aware of the enemy they were facing: "The battle is not yours, but God's."[7]

In this passage of Scripture, God reassures King Jehoshaphat that the battle is not Israel's to fight. Instead, it is God's battle, and God reigns undefeated, meaning He has not lost a battle and will never lose one. Still, God tells the Israelites to march down against their enemies—right after He tells them it's not even their battle to fight.

Why do the Israelites have to show up to the battle when they were told it's not theirs in the first place?

I believe the answer to this question is found in verse 17. God wants us to be on the battlefield, not so that we get attacked or fight or hurt. God wants us on the battlefield so that we can *see deliverance.*

My husband tells the story of the best game he ever saw in person. Alabama, his alma mater, was playing Clemson in the NCAA National Championship in 2016. The game was a constant battle—back and forth throughout the four quarters. But, in the end, Alabama scored and went ahead, winning the game. Austin describes the stadium's energy and the fans cheering with the same enthusiasm a little kid might tell you about the new bike they got for Christmas. It was an incredible thing for Austin to *experience* a victory.

Now, I, on the other hand, was not there for the game. And while I'm an Alabama fan, too, because I was not there in person, I can't relate to the feeling of the victory like Austin can. I can listen to Austin tell the story and be happy that he had a great experience, but I can't account for it myself because I wasn't there.

And I think this is why God wants us to see deliverance for ourselves. It's one thing to witness a miracle in someone else's life, but it's an entirely different thing to witness a miracle in your life. However, victories only come with battles, and battles often come with fear, so to win, you must overcome your fear and show up to the fight.

Luckily for us, we already have the victory! There are no guessing games or wondering who will win. Anytime we find ourselves battling it out or attacked by Satan, we know from the beginning that we win, not because of anything we've done but because of the victory Jesus won on the cross.

We must pursue awareness of the enemy's schemes because we are all required to be on the battlefield of spiritual warfare. It comes with the territory. And at this point, you may be asking, "What is spiritual warfare? What does this look like?" I think this verse explains the process of spiritual warfare beautifully:

"For our struggle is not against flesh and blood, but against the rulers, against the authorities, against the powers of this dark world and against the spiritual forces of evil in the heavenly realms." - Ephesians 6:12 NIV

On top of understanding the different schemes of the enemy, we must also know the following about spiritual warfare:

1. Our fights are not against people.
2. Our fights are against the rulers, authorities, and powers of the dark world.

3. There are spiritual forces of evil in the heavenly realms.
4. There are also spiritual forces of good in the heavenly realms, and these forces *always win*.

We may be tempted to picture the "battlefield" as our workplace, social media, church, or home. Often, we want to picture our enemy as our boss, spouse, parents, neighbors, or politicians. But Ephesians 6:12 makes it clear that our battlefield and enemies are not against *flesh and blood*, meaning they are not people or places we can see.

Instead, our battlefield and enemies are in the heavenly realms, the spirits and places we cannot see. This means that showing up to the battlefield is not us fighting with the people we're mad at or simply taking steps to defend ourselves physically. We show up to the battlefield through prayer, worship, and biblical community. Because here's the deal: **All warfare is spiritual warfare.**

HOW DO I PURSUE AWARENESS?

"Be alert and of sober mind. Your enemy prowls around like a roaring lion looking for someone to devour. Resist him, standing firm in the faith, because you know that the family of believers throughout the world is undergoing the same kind of sufferings."
1 Peter 5:8-9 NIV

You may be thinking, "I'm not at war with anyone! I just don't like my boss." Maybe you're thinking, "I don't want to fight anyone! I just want that person to apologize for how they treated me in the store."

No matter what conflict you're experiencing in your life, it's warfare. However, without the proper awareness of the enemy's schemes, you'll find yourself fighting a losing battle because you'll find yourself fighting the *wrong* battle. People aren't your problem. Satan is your problem.

Awareness happens gradually, and it is a never-ending process. We know that we have an enemy, and we must be aware of his schemes to know the actual battles we're facing. But how do we become aware of the battles going on around us? The outline for how to pursue awareness is found in 1 Peter 5:8-9.

Resist the enemy.

1 Peter 5:8-9 tells us to "be alert and of sober mind. Your enemy prowls around like a roaring lion looking for someone to devour. Resist him…"

When pursuing awareness, we first and foremost must resist the enemy. "Resist" in the original Greek means to "withstand" or "oppose."[8] When we resist the enemy, we take steps to withstand his attacks and oppose his ways. Here's a classic verse on resisting the enemy:

"Submit yourselves, then, to God. Resist the devil, and he will flee from you."
- James 4:7 NIV

We cannot resist the enemy until we submit to God. Remember how we said that Satan does have some power? Without being adequately submitted to God and His authority, we won't be able to withstand or oppose the devil or his demons. However, when we are submitted to God, resting under His authority and Word, we are unstoppable to the spiritual forces of darkness. We resist the enemy, withstand, and oppose his works by submitting to the Lord.

Submission to God looks like asking Him to be in control and yielding to His Word. We can accomplish this through prayer, worship, and reading our Bibles. Our trust and faith will grow as we take these steps to submit to God. When we submit to God and resist the enemy, he will flee!

Rest on faith.

1 Peter 5:9 continues, "Resist him, standing firm in your faith." The word "faith" is the Greek word *pistis*. *Pistis* is the "conviction that God exists and is the creator and ruler of all things, the provider and bestower of eternal salvation through Christ."[9] When we call our faith to mind, when we remember that God exists and that He is the Creator and Ruler of everything, when we know that God is our Provider and Bestower of salvation and that heaven is our home, the things that seem to steal, kill, and destroy on this earth don't seem so big anymore. We are reminded that the enemy is not as big as we think he is.

When we rest on faith, we choose to focus on faith. Instead of believing the enemy's lies or giving in to our fear, we focus on the awesome God we serve and His power. Remember: fear is an attack on focus. As we rest in faith, our focus shifts from our fear to our Father. The more we rest on faith, the more we remind ourselves how big our God is!

Rely on community.

1 Peter 5:9 closes with this: "Resist him, standing firm in the faith, because you know that the family of believers throughout the world is undergoing the same kind of sufferings."

One of the greatest gifts God gave humanity, besides Jesus, was community. We see in Genesis that God created Eve to commune with Adam. We see in the life of Jesus that He had disciples who traveled and did life with Him. If Jesus prioritized community, then we should, too.

The phrase "family of believers" in 1 Peter 5 applies to all Christians. All believers in Jesus struggle, strive, and sin. Therefore, all believers in Jesus need the support of community. Don't get trapped in the "poor me" cycle. The pity party must end.

1 Peter 5:9 tells us that a *family* of believers is going through the same kind of suffering. That means that whatever you're facing, somewhere, there is a believer who knows *exactly* how you feel. In fact, Jesus Himself knows how you feel! If someone else knows how you feel, then this person can likely give you a different perspective on the same situation—and a change in perspective will always help you become more aware.

You are not alone. Get around people who can encourage you and are willing to share their stories with you. Seek out mentors who will give you godly wisdom. Find people who are walking through similar circumstances as you. Get around people you can mentor and pour into them.

God never meant for us to be weak, and God never meant for us to be lonely. When we realize we're not alone, we feel empowered, making us more aware of the miracle-working God we serve, and this awareness will help us fight the enemy.

As we resist the enemy, rest on faith, and rely on community, we pursue awareness daily, not only of the enemy's schemes but also of the power and strength of our God! What we used to classify as "coincidences" will no longer be so. What we used to let bother us will no longer frustrate us. We will have a firm understanding that we have an enemy, but no, we will not be defeated in Jesus's Name!

Daily Declaration

"I understand that my friends, family members, co-workers, and acquaintances are not my enemies. I know I have one enemy who only exists to steal, kill, and destroy, and his name is Satan. I know that Satan has schemes, but I choose to be aware of those schemes today. I also choose to be aware of the victory Jesus has won for me on the cross so I will not fear. I will resist the enemy, rest on faith, and rely on community. Ultimately, I will overcome the enemy by the

blood of Jesus and the word of my testimony! I am not a loser. I am a winner in Jesus's Name!"

PURSUE DAILY

10

PURSUE YOUR GIFTING

"For this reason I remind you to fan into flame the gift of God, which is in you through the laying on of my hands."
2 Timothy 1:6 NIV

GIFTS THAT KEEP GIVING

What's the best gift you've ever received? Can you picture it? Maybe you're looking at it or using it right now. Perhaps you can see it in a distant memory from when you were a child. It could be a bike, doll house, or kitchen appliance (if you're domestic like me). It could be a new phone, a car, or a lifetime trip. It's fun to think about those gifts, right?

Now, think with me for a second about the gifts you've received that, well, weren't the best. The gifts that you opened and had to hide your actual reaction for fear of hurting someone's feelings. The gifts that make you ask, "How did this person ever think this was something I would want?" I'm sure we all have had a few of these in our lifetime, and let's be honest, these gifts are still awesome because they give us a great laugh!

I can't quite tell you what my favorite gift is that I've received. It's between my car, engagement ring, thoughtful flowers, a card from a friend, and my InstantPot. Yes, the InstantPot is up there because, remember, I am domestic. Also, a Hamilton Beach Single-serve blender. It was the staple of Christmas 2016.

We all have gifts that we remember, and what makes them memorable is the experience that came with them. Gifts that made our lives easier. Gifts that brought joy to our lives. Gifts that gave us a good laugh. Gifts that were, in one way or another, put to use.

The gifts that tend to be forgotten are the ones that are set aside or returned—the ones that we never used or cared to use. These gifts leave little to no impact on our hearts or minds because they never became a part of our lives. In our eyes, they were unworthy of our time and attention, so we discarded them and moved on. Out of sight, out of mind.

What if I told you that some of the greatest gifts you'd ever receive were sitting in your living room right now, waiting to be opened? What if I told you that priceless, life-changing gifts were just a few steps away, and all you had to do was receive them?

What if I told you that, unfortunately for many of us, there are some of the greatest gifts we'll ever receive inside of us right now, but because we think we're unworthy or don't have time for them, we fail to open them? Remember what happens to gifts that fail to be put to use? They are forgotten.

These gifts, spiritual gifts, are specifically designed for you. They're the most personalized and priceless gifts you'll ever receive. The gifting God has put inside you is specific to your person, personality, and story. It doesn't matter if you have 100 friends with the same Enneagram number as you and are all interested in the same things. It doesn't matter that everyone in your degree program seems to be interested in the same field and performing the same way. It doesn't matter that, in your eyes, you don't see how you'll ever be able to stand out or be noticed. Your gifting is different. Your gifting is individual, and that makes you special.

Special gifts get noticed. Special gifts get used. Special gifts are perfect. And according to James 1:17, "Every good and perfect gift is from above, coming down from the Father of the heavenly lights, who does not change like shifting shadows."
Have you identified your spiritual gifts? Have you unwrapped them? Have you put them to use? As we go through this chapter together, we will discover just how special God made you and how you can pursue your gifting daily to accomplish the good and perfect purpose God designed you to fulfill!

WHAT ARE SPIRITUAL GIFTS?

"God has given each of you a gift from His great variety of spiritual gifts. Use them well to serve one another."
1 Peter 4:10 NLT

Depending on what type of church you've attended, you may or may not be familiar with spiritual gifts. The word "gift" in our theme verse for this section means "a favor with which one receives without any merit of his own."[1] A "spiritual gift" is not something spooky, scary, or freaky. A spiritual gift is simply a gift or talent God has given you. This gift or talent is not something that you earned or created; instead, it is something that's been given to you freely by God. He has given you favor to succeed in a specific area.

The word "gift" can also refer to "grace or gifts denoting extraordinary powers, distinguishing certain Christians and enabling them to serve the church of Christ."[2] When this definition mentions "powers," it's not talking about something that will turn you into Iron Man or Captain Marvel (although that would be pretty cool!). Spiritual gifts give you the power and ability to serve others, as 1 Peter 4:10 tells us. In all, spiritual gifts are divine talents that God has supernaturally given us so that we can be equipped to do what He has called us to do.

There are many opinions on "how many" spiritual gifts there are in the Bible. In 1 Corinthians 12, Paul lists out nine spiritual gifts. Ephesians 4:11-12 lists five spiritual gifts. Romans 12:6-8 lists seven spiritual gifts. Which list is correct? Which list can we use to define our spiritual gifting?

All of them. While these passages of Scripture may list different or similar spiritual gifts, they do not invalidate each other but complement each other. If you look at all three chapters and the gifts displayed, you end up with this collective list:

- Apostleship (Ephesians 4:11)
- Discernment (1 Corinthians 12:10)
- Encouragement (Romans 12:8)
- Evangelism (Ephesians 4:11)
- Faith (1 Corinthians 12:9)
- Giving (Romans 12:8)
- Healing (1 Corinthians 12:9)
- Interpretation of Tongues (1 Corinthians 12:10)
- Knowledge (1 Corinthians 12:8)
- Leadership (Romans 12:8)
- Mercy (Romans 12:8)
- Miracles (1 Corinthians 12:10)

- Prophecy (1 Corinthians 12:10; Romans 12:6; Ephesians 4:11)
- Pastor/shepherd (Ephesians 4:11)
- Serving (Romans 12:7)
- Teaching (Romans 12:7; Ephesians 4:11)
- Tongues (1 Corinthians 12:10)
- Wisdom (1 Corinthians 12:8)

These three chapters that speak specifically to spiritual gifts comprise 18 spiritual gifts. Does that mean these are the only gifts you can have? Does this mean that you must fit into one of these categories? I would dare to say no. This answer comes from 1 Peter 4:10, which states that God gives us gifts from His "great variety of spiritual gifts." I don't know about you, but I can't imagine that 18 is a "great variety" to God. I mean, come on. He's *God*. I know of humans that have more than 18 cars. If humans can have 18 as a "great variety," God's variety is much larger!

The point is this: We shouldn't get bogged down about how many gifts there are or what exactly they are. The important thing is to look at yourself and evaluate:

- Who am I?
- What do I enjoy?
- What am I good at?
- What is my calling?
- Why am I here?
- What am I passionate about?
- What keeps me up at night?
- What would I sacrifice everything for?

Do you know the answer to the questions above? If you do, you're well on your way to understanding your spiritual gifts. If you're reading the words "calling" and "passionate" and don't know what I'm talking about, hang in there—this chapter is for you. God created you with a specific purpose, and He's equipped you to fulfill that purpose through spiritual gifts![3]

WHY DO I NEED SPIRITUAL GIFTS?

"For just as each of us has one body with many members, and these members do not all have the same function, so in Christ, though many, form one body, and each member belongs to all the others. We have different gifts, according to the grace given each of us."
Romans 12:4-6 NIV

Hopefully, by now, you're starting to desire to learn your spiritual gifts and how to use them. However, before we discuss the "how," we must answer a critical question: Why do we even *need* spiritual gifts? If it's something that you're going to be pursuing daily, you must know why you're pursuing it.

Paul paints a beautiful picture in Romans 12 that shows the importance of the individual in the Church by comparing it to a body. As Romans 12 lays out, each of us has different gifts given to us by God.[4] Just as our bodies have different parts that work together, the Church is made up of different people who work together. Each person has a specific job to do. If a part of our body were missing or not functioning correctly, our entire body would be affected.

In 2018, I had a bad ear infection in my right ear. There was so much inflammation and fluid trapped that I could barely hear out of that ear, and my balance was off. It also caused severe headaches and earaches, and I dealt with these issues for months. When people would ask what was wrong, I hated to tell them, "It's my ear." It's such a small part of my body that I thought no one would take it seriously. It's not like I had the flu, strep throat, or something else "more serious." It was just my ear.

While my ear is a small part of my body, it affected my entire body and lifestyle when it wasn't functioning correctly. In the same way, you may think that your role in the Kingdom of God is so small that no one will even care. You may feel your part to play isn't worth your time or anyone else's. But I'm here to tell you that *every* part, even the smallest one, has something to accomplish, and if it's not fulfilled, it's noticed.

This train of thought brings us to this idea: It's not necessarily about what your gifts can do for you but rather about what your gifts can do for God. When we know our gifts and how we were made, we can serve in the areas that align with our purpose. When we're operating at full capacity, doing all the things God created and designed us to do, we are in the middle of His good, pleasing, and perfect will.[5] However, when we're not using our gifts and pursuing what God has for us, we're not being obedient.

I had this thought a few weeks ago in church when our senior pastor was preaching about doing what we were created to do. I found myself constantly assessing whether my gifts were "worth" using based on how much money I could make or how many followers I could get on social media. I assessed my success in book sales, opportunities to speak publicly, and the number of times people looked to me for advice. And God, in His gentle but confrontational love, revealed to me that that is a twisted way of thinking.

At the end of our lives, when we stand before God in heaven, we won't give an account for how much money we made or how many Instagram followers we had. We will not be accountable for how many views we got on TikTok or how many listens our podcast received. We won't be accountable for how many goals or points we scored or how many 100s we got on tests. What we will be held accountable for is if we were *faithful* in using the gifts God gave us. We'll be held responsible for our obedience.

Jesus shares a parable in Matthew 25 called "The Parable of the Bags of Gold."[6] In this story, there is a master who gives three servants three different amounts of talents (which is money, but interesting translation, don't you think?). Each servant goes off and does different things with what they were given. One servant didn't do anything with his talents and was reprimanded. Another invested his talents and made more, and the master responded with this: "Well done, good and faithful servant!"[7]

This parable symbolizes the interaction we'll have with God in heaven. We aim to hear the words, "Well done, good and faithful servant!" The only way we can hear these words is to use what God has given us, not hide it away.

So, what's your dream? What's your purpose? What do you believe God has called you to do? Are you being obedient to it, or are you allowing fear to hold you back? Ultimately, pursuing your spiritual gifting is an act of obedience, and using your gifts will bring you fulfillment and, most importantly, bring glory to God.

HOW DO I PURSUE SPIRITUAL GIFTS?

"For this reason I remind you to fan into flame the gift of God, which is in you through the laying on of my hands."
2 Timothy 1:6 NIV

Throughout this chapter, we've discussed what spiritual gifts are and why we need them. Now, it's time to discuss how we receive and pursue spiritual gifts.

Receiving Spiritual Gifts

Naturally, our spiritual gifts come from God. That's what makes them spiritual *gifts*. These gifts weren't talents we got to pick when we were born. Your parents didn't submit a form and say, "We want a child that can do _____." Even if you argue that you get some of your talents from your parents, who did they get their gifts from? Their parents? Then, who did their parents get their skills from? The list goes on and on, and eventually, it ends with God. God is the one who gives us our gifts. Jeremiah 1:5 says God "knit" us together in our mothers' wombs. He formed us, piece by piece. He knew the gifts you would need to accomplish your purpose, and He gave them to you.

Even though we are initially gifted with certain things by God, we can also ask God for more spiritual gifts throughout our Christian life. 1 Corinthians 14:1 says to "follow the way of love and eagerly desire gifts of the Spirit." The word "desire" in the original language can be translated to "pursue."[8] The Bible *literally* tells us to pursue spiritual gifts! If you're not good at something you want to be good at, ask God for talent. If you want the gift of leadership, teaching, or discernment, ask God for that gift. However, be sure to pursue additional gifts only with the heart that you're adding to your variety of gifts, not replacing them. It's a sign of maturity to seek additional gifts, but it's a sign of insecurity to ask for an entirely new set of gifts. Remember, whatever you were designed to do was specifically *for you*, so don't be so eager to become someone else. God gave you your gifts so you could be who He created you to be!

So, now that we've discussed a few ways we can receive spiritual gifts, let's talk about what to do next. How do we pursue spiritual gifts?

Pursuing Spiritual Gifts

If you don't know your spiritual gifts, I encourage you to review the list we discussed earlier in this chapter. Those are the spiritual gifts that are explicitly mentioned in the Bible. Go through the list and see which ones could apply to you. However, as we said, many other gifts have been identified and interpreted through Scripture, like administration, worship, etc. Therefore, I encourage you to take a spiritual gift assessment online or at your local church if offered. Be sure to run the assessment by a trusted spiritual authority to ensure it's biblically accurate before you take it.

If you know your spiritual gifts, the Bible encourages you in 2 Timothy 2:6 to "fan into flame the gift of God." Have you ever fanned a flame before? When you start a fire, it starts small. There's a lot of smoke and not a lot of flame. However, the more you care for and kindle it, the bigger and brighter it gets.

Just as professional athletes still practice daily, we must strengthen and pursue our gifts daily for optimal use. We must "kindle" our gifts. Some of them may start rocky. You may not know what to do with them or how to use them, but the more you work on and strengthen your gifts, the better they will be.

As you continue to pursue your gifting daily, you will be well on your way to putting your God-given gifts into action. Only then will you be able to fulfill your purpose and live the life God always intended for you here on earth!

Daily Declaration

"I know God has given me unique spiritual gifts. I did not earn these gifts. Instead, they have been freely given to me by God to accomplish a specific purpose. Therefore, I commit to pursuing my gifting daily. I will work to develop these gifts so that I can be ready to fulfill the plan God has for me. Thank you, God, for choosing me!

PURSUE DAILY

11

PURSUE HEALTH

"Beloved, I pray that in all respects you may prosper and be in good health, just as your soul prospers."
3 John 1:2 NASB

HEART SICK

"This is going to be the best weekend."

As Austin and I pulled up to a classy resort in Orlando one weekend for a marriage retreat, this is what I thought. The resort was massive and beautiful. There were chocolate-covered strawberries in our room. Everything we wanted and needed was at our fingertips.

We had an interesting couple of months leading up to this trip, and we were both excited for a relaxing and restful weekend with some other couples from our church.

We sat through a meeting and then went to dinner that night at a high-end restaurant at the resort. We had two or three courses before the main course came. I cut into my steak and took a bite. *Delectable.* I took another bite, and suddenly, I felt like I was going to pass out. I looked at my Apple Watch, and my heart rate was 40 BPM. Then, I looked down again, and when my watch refreshed, my heart rate was at 140 BPM.

My heart rate kept increasing, and I got short of breath. I tapped Austin's shoulder in a panic until I got his attention. As I was tapping him, my vision started getting blurry, and the noise around me died down. I was losing my sight and hearing, and I thought I was going to die, which made me panic even more.

Austin could tell something was wrong. The people at the table immediately began to pray over me. As we started praying, my heart rate slowed, and my body started shaking from the adrenaline. It took me some time to collect myself after a scare like that. At the end, I thought, "That was so weird, but I'm glad it's over!"

The following day, we were sitting in a conference room with the other couples for the retreat. Austin is speaking, and I get the same feeling I had at dinner. I grabbed his arm, and, again, he could tell something wasn't right. My heart rate had spiked to 170 BPM, and we headed to the hospital.

Tests and needles and machines and hours of waiting later, we had no answers. Praise God everything looked fine on paper! But my heart was still not settled. I could tell something was very wrong. I was alive, though, and that's what was most important.

Over the next few weeks, my heart slowly got better, but I still had episodes about once a day. On the days I didn't have episodes, I found myself waiting to have one, expecting it to happen when I least thought it would. I hated the feeling of being caught off guard, so if I was expecting my heart rate to skyrocket, I couldn't be surprised, right?

The truth is this *whole situation* caught me off guard. Because my physical heart appeared healthy, everyone asked about my emotional and mental health. "Are you anxious? Are you stressed?" they would ask. I would respond with a resolute "no" because I didn't think anything was off. Austin and I were at a resort on an all-expenses paid trip when this occurred. Does that sound stressful to anyone else?

However, through months of prayer and doctor's visits, I finally realized that God was teaching me something through this situation. I don't believe God caused my heart and body to be sick, but I do believe He used it to teach me a lesson. And here's the lesson I learned: Even if my heart looked good on the outside and I couldn't identify any emotional or mental triggers for my heart to act the way it did, somewhere, somehow, I had become unhealthy.

Now, thank God, I am completely healed of that issue! However, this incident taught me how to dig deep and examine my life. Was I stressed, and I didn't know it? Was I running at a pace that my heart couldn't handle? Was the emotional toll of ministry too much for how I was trying to process it? It sent me spiraling—in a good way. It got me thinking outside of the box. It got me prioritizing my health in ways I hadn't even considered.

I learned that, sometimes, being unhealthy is something that happens to you. You get a diagnosis that shocks you. You catch a cold or virus from someone at work or school. Your heart rate skyrockets while you're eating a steak, and no one can explain why. You didn't cause the unhealthiness. It just happened.

But I also learned that, sometimes, being unhealthy is a byproduct of the choices we make. We get tired and sick because we're living at an unsustainable pace. Our social lives are a wreck because we're scared of being hurt. Our spiritual health is lacking because we don't make time to be with God.

If you're experiencing disease or illness, I fully believe that God can *and* will ultimately heal you because His Word says that by Jesus's wounds, you are healed![1] However, this chapter on health is dedicated to the areas we control, the areas where sickness has occurred as a product of choices we've made. So, let's talk about living a healthy life as best we can by pursuing health daily.

WHAT IS HEALTH?

"Beloved, I pray that in all respects you may prosper and be in good health, just as your soul prospers."
3 John 1:2 NASB

"Health" is a popular word in our society today. Paired with words like "mental" and "emotional," the word "health" can be seen or mentioned on basically any media platform and in any spiritual conversation. As we can see in the theme verse for this chapter, this obsession and, dare I say, *necessary desire* for health is biblical. In 3 John 1:2, John writes to a man named Gaius[2] and says that he's praying for him to prosper in all respects and be in good health, just as his "soul prospers."[3]

But what is this "health" that John is talking about? Is it congruent with the health we desire for our bodies, minds, and emotions? Is it health that we can achieve from eating, sleeping, and exercising well, or is this health something deeper?

The original word for "health" in 3 John 1:2 means "to be sound, to be well, [or] to be in good health."[4] While it is difficult to discern what "health" problems, if any, Gaius was facing, it is clear that John was concerned with more than Gaius's physical health. In the same verse, he writes about Gaius's soul and even says he wants him to be healthy in "all respects."[5] Therefore, one can deduce that John is praying for health in *all* areas for his friend—not just his physical health. John is praying for Gaius to experience health in his emotions, relationships, spirituality, finances—you name it! John (and I would also say *Jesus*) desires us to have lives that are filled with health!

Psalm 103 encourages us to "forget not all His benefits" that the Lord would give His people in salvation.[6] Here's a list of these benefits:

- Forgiveness
- Healing
- Redemption
- Love and compassion
- Satisfaction[7]

Included in that list? Healing! This means that health is already available to us through the cross of Jesus Christ. Even so, we still must do our part to live healthy lives daily. So, what does this look like? Let's begin with the areas of health.

If you search "areas of health" or "types of health" online, you get a lot of answers. You get a variety of lists, and honestly, it's challenging to know which one is correct. However, throughout most of the lists, five areas of health hold true:

- Physical health
- Emotional health
- Social health
- Spiritual health
- Mental health

I'm no scientist or health specialist, but I believe we can find each of these areas of health in the Bible, and that's why this is the list I chose to include in this book. After all, God made our bodies, emotions, community needs, spirits, and brains. Therefore, one must believe He wants us to take care of them! As we continue in this journey of pursuing health together, keep these five key areas in mind. Here's a brief explanation of each area of health and where you can see it in the Bible:

Physical Health
"For while bodily training is of some value, godliness is of value in every way, as it holds promise for the present life and also for the life to come." - 1 Timothy 4:8 ESV

Our physical health focuses on our bodies. 1 Corinthians 6:19 says our "bodies are temples of the Holy Spirit." We see in 1 Timothy 4:8 that while the body isn't the most important thing, it is of "some value" to pay attention to our physical needs and train our bodies. Our physical health includes exercise, sleep, eating well, and anything else that can help our physical bodies thrive.

Emotional Health
"Beloved, I pray that in all respects you may prosper and be in good health, just as your soul prospers." - 3 John 1:2 NASB

3 John 1:2 says that our "souls" must prosper. Instead of titling this section "emotional" health, I could've simply titled it "soul" health. The word "soul" in this verse is the word *psychē*, which represents our "feelings, desires, affections, [and] aversions."[8] In other words, it represents our heart. Our emotions, in reality, are symptoms of a deeper issue. Often, those issues are found in our hearts. Proverbs 4:23 says, "Above all else, guard your heart, for everything you do flows from it." Everything we feel, say, and do flows from our hearts. Therefore, our emotional health is essential.

Social Health

"Every day they continued to meet together in the temple courts. They broke bread in their homes and ate together with glad and sincere hearts, praising God and enjoying the favor of all the people. And the Lord added to their number daily those who were being saved." - Acts 2:46-47 NIV

The Book of Acts in the Bible is all about Christians figuring out their flow. A massive part of this "life" as Christians involves fellowship and social gatherings. We can see clearly in Jesus's ministry that he valued social health. Jesus desired to be by Himself at certain times, but He also spent a lot of time with other people. After Jesus was resurrected and ascended to heaven, His disciples kept meeting with other people and building godly community. Therefore, if social health was an essential part of the early Church, we can assume it is an integral part of the Church today.

Spiritual Health

"A cheerful heart is good medicine, but a crushed spirit dries up the bones." - Proverbs 17:22 NIV

This one shouldn't need much explanation. God cares about our spirits. Proverbs 17:22 says that a "crushed spirit dries up the bones." In other words, a crushed spirit brings illness. If our spirits are down and out, so is our health. Our spiritual health includes our relationship with God, His Word, and His Church.

Mental Health

"For God has not given us a spirit of fear, but of power and of love and of a sound mind." - 2 Timothy 1:7 NKJV

According to 2 Timothy 1:7, God desires us to have a sound mind! He wants us to have a *peaceful* and *controlled* mind. The original word for "sound mind" is *sōphronismos*, which means "soundness of mind" or "moderation and self-control."[9] God does not desire for us to live in fear, anxiety, worry, doubt, or illness of the mind. Instead, God wants us to have a mind governed by life and peace.[10]

WHY SHOULD I PURSUE HEALTH?
"Do you not know that your bodies are temples of the Holy Spirit, who is in you, whom you have received from God? You are not your own; you were bought at a price. Therefore honor God with your bodies."
1 Corinthians 6:19-20 NIV

After discussing the different areas of health and what they mean for you and me, I hope you desire to be healthy in every way. I hope you, as 3 John 1:2 says, desire to "prosper." However, if you need a little more convincing to live a healthy lifestyle, let's discuss why, as a Christian, you need to pursue health.

The most important reason we need to be healthy is that the Bible says to honor God with our bodies.[11] This "honor" doesn't simply mean we have to take care of our physical bodies. It also honors God when we care for our spirits and souls. In other words, one of the best ways to honor God is by being healthy in every area—physically, emotionally, socially, spiritually, and mentally.

The second (and most practical) reason we need to be healthy is that, without health, we can't get anything done! I don't know about you, but I want to live for the Lord and win people for Him until I'm 120. Living long, full lives doesn't happen by accident. It happens by choices that we make *today*. When we choose to take care of our physical, emotional, social, spiritual, and mental health, we are making choices today that influence our ability to serve the Lord tomorrow.

Finally, we must remember that our bodies are borrowed property. Therefore, the way that we take care of them matters.

Have you ever let someone borrow something that mattered to you? Maybe it was your car or phone. Perhaps it was a clothing item. Maybe it was some money. When someone borrows from you, whatever the item may be, chances are you expect to receive the borrowed item back in the same or *better* condition than when you lent it.

1 Corinthians 6:19-20 makes it clear that we are not our own; instead, we were bought at a price through the ransom of Jesus.[12] Did you know that your body and life aren't actually yours? You're not the owner. You are the steward.

Romans 6:23 says that the "wages of sin are death." This verse means that there is a cost to sinning, and that cost is death. When Jesus died on the cross, He brought us "redemption through His blood, the forgiveness of sins."[13] In other words, when Jesus died on the cross, He paid our debt. The cost for sinning was death, and He paid it with His life. Therefore, we now belong to Him, and since we belong to Him, we must *live* as though we belong to Him. When we realize that we're living in borrowed property with borrowed air, pursuing health means we want to make the most of the bodies, souls, and spirits God has given us.

HOW DO I PURSUE HEALTH?

"Therefore confess your sins to each other and pray for each other so that you may be healed. The prayer of a righteous person is powerful and effective."
James 5:16 NIV

We have established thus far that the Bible has a lot to say about our health. We know God wants us to be healthy in our spirits, souls, and bodies. So, how do we get healthy?

The answer to this question is simple: We get healthy through healing.

As much as Scripture discusses "health," it has more to say about healing. God repeatedly promises that healing is readily available to us. Isaiah 53:5 says that Jesus "was pierced for our transgressions, He was crushed for our iniquities; the punishment that brought us peace was on Him, and by His wounds, we are healed." Therefore, because Jesus died on the cross for us, we *are* healed—present tense.

Jesus's sacrifice on the cross resulted in complete, total, and *immediate* healing for us in every area of our lives. Sometimes, however, this healing doesn't show up right away or in the way we think it should. If God promises that we are healed, then *we are healed*, but a healthy life and healing are things we must pursue. This does not mean that our illness or pain is always our fault. This means we have to partner with God in our healing process to see health in our physical, emotional, social, spiritual, and mental lives.

So, before we talk about how to get healthy, here are three things you need to know about the healing process.

Healing is messy.

Think about the incisions, bleeding, disease, and infection that can happen during surgery. Even though the facility is spotless and the doctor performing your surgery is well-trained, you can't argue that the healing process isn't messy. If someone is in triage at the hospital and dying, they don't care if their clothes get messed up or if there's blood everywhere. They don't care about the mess. They just want to *live*.

In the same way, we should not be concerned about the appearance of our healing process. Some situations or emotions will shock us in the process of healing. Sometimes, there will be moments that are unplanned and imperfect. And *that's okay*. In the end, we shouldn't care how messy the process is. We just want to *live* in all areas of our lives, so we're willing to deal with the temporary mess for eternal healing.

Healing is painful.

I hate pain. In fact, I *fear* pain. I avoid pain as much as possible, and I believe I'm not alone in this avoidance. I also think this is why many people avoid the healing process. We're afraid of the pain of healing.

Have you heard the saying, "It has to get worse before it gets better"? I don't think that's necessarily biblical, but it can be true. Along with our hospital analogy, consider someone who comes in and needs emergency surgery. They need an incision to be made stat to save their life, and they don't have time for anesthesia. Will this move be painful? Yes. But will this move bring healing? Yes.

Sometimes, God must open a wound to heal it, and the opening and treatment of that wound can be painful. It can bring up past experiences and emotions that we thought were long gone (or that we tried our best to bury but still feel every day). Healing can cause us to feel the pain of release, but it will also cause us to feel the peace of freedom. Don't shy away from the pain of healing. The peace on the other side is worth the pain.

Healing is necessary.

In the end, if we want to truly live, we must be healed. We must submit to the healing process. What is not healed will kill. And while it may not physically kill us, it can destroy our hopes, dreams, quality of life, and joy.

Understand that healing is *necessary* to live the life God has called you to live. While we may think avoiding the issues will bring healing, that is not true; when we avoid problems, we maintain them instead of healing them. You don't "maintain" sickness. You work to overcome sickness—and praise God that He has already overcome it for us!

What you shove under the rug will not stay hidden forever. Everything will eventually come to light. The quicker you get to healing, the more of your life you take back from the enemy, and the faster you get back on track to living out your God-given purpose.

Healing is messy. Healing is painful. But healing is *necessary*. Pursuing health is essential to our lives as believers in Jesus. Again, while we believe in God's Word for healing, we also have a part to play in the healing process. For each area of health (physical, emotional, social, spiritual, and mental) you are pursuing, pray and ask God to reveal how you can take active steps to improve in those areas. Start with one practical step you can take daily to pursue health in your physical, emotional, social, spiritual, and mental life. Maybe it's getting adequate sleep. Maybe it's spending the first twenty minutes of your day in prayer and worship. Maybe it's planning to hang out with a friend once a week. Whatever steps you decide to take, *actually take them* to pursue health daily.

All of the above are examples of steps you can take to pursue health. However, James 5:16 makes it clear that there are two essential steps to the healing process. Regardless of which area you're pursuing health in, make sure these steps are a priority:

Confess your sins and receive prayer.

Healing is not a solo sport. To truly heal, you must have people in your life who you can be honest with. While the phrase "confess your sins" may seem daunting, what the Bible is really telling us to do is to tell someone the truth. When we "confess," we acknowledge openly where we've done something wrong or allowed something inside of us that's not supposed to be there.[14] Anywhere we've sinned or are unhealthy could be an area where we have had a "lapse...from truth and uprightness."[15]

Again, sometimes, the unhealthiness we're experiencing has nothing to do with our choices. Still, for the areas where our unhealthiness is our own doing, we must share with others honestly and openly about where we're at and what we're feeling. From there, who we confide in can pray for us specifically. These people we confess to and seek prayer from can be professional counselors, pastors, trusted friends or family members, or church groups. We will discuss the importance of godly community and how to pursue it in the next chapter.

Pray for others' healing.

James 5:16 tells us to "confess [our] sins to each other and pray for each other so that [we] may be healed," as we just mentioned in the previous step. A lot of churches use this verse to support their small group ministries by saying that healing comes from confessing to one another and receiving prayer, which is true. However, this verse does not say to confess our sins and simply *receive* prayer from someone. On the contrary, this verse says to "pray for each other," and healing will occur.[16]

Could it be that, sometimes, our healing is one prayer away, but instead of being a prayer for *ourselves*, it's a prayer for *others*? There is something powerful about praying for others to experience what you want to experience for yourself. According to James 5:16, praying for others is essential to pursuing health.

Whatever you're praying for—physical, emotional, social, spiritual, or mental healing—may I encourage you to pray for someone else to experience the outcome you desire for yourself? This does not mean you forfeit your right and ability to receive healing yourself; God is limitless, which means there is plenty of healing to go around! Praying this way gets your focus off your problem and allows you to focus on someone else. And who knows? God may use the prayer you pray for someone else to heal you! After all, "the prayer of a righteous person is powerful and effective."[17]

By now, I pray that you believe God wants to heal you. I pray that you know God desires for you to be healthy in all areas of your life and that health requires our participation. Yes, healing is messy and painful, but it's also a necessary process that will allow us to live the lives God always intended for us if we submit to it.

Revelation 12:11 says we overcome the enemy by the "blood of the Lamb and by the word of [our] testimony."[18] To truly overcome our issues and illnesses, we must know what God's Word says about healing. We must know about the blood of Jesus and remind the enemy (and ourselves) about what God has done in our lives this far. As we close out this chapter, take note of these verses and hold onto them as a beacon of hope in your healing process.

- "Heal me, Lord, and I will be healed; save me and I will be saved, for you are the one I praise." (Jeremiah 17:14)
- "Is anyone among you sick? Let them call the elders of the church to pray over them and anoint them with oil in the name of the Lord. And the prayer offered in faith will make the sick person well; the Lord will raise them up. If they have sinned, they will be forgiven." (James 5:14-15)
- "But He was pierced for our transgressions, He was crushed for our iniquities; the punishment that brought us peace was on Him, and by His wounds we are healed." (Isaiah 53:5)
- "So do not fear, for I am with you; do not be dismayed, for I am your God. I will strengthen you and help you; I will uphold you with my righteous right hand." (Isaiah 41:10)

- "'But I will restore you to health and heal your wounds,' declares the Lord, 'because you are called an outcast, Zion for whom no one cares.'" (Jeremiah 30:17)
- "And my God will meet all your needs according to the riches of His glory in Christ Jesus." (Philippians 4:19)
- "He will wipe every tear from their eyes. There will be no more death, or mourning or crying or pain, for the old order of things has passed away." (Revelation 21:4)

Daily Declaration

"I believe God wants me to be healed in every way. He wants me to be whole and complete physically, emotionally, spiritually, socially, and mentally. I choose to pursue health in every area of my life. I will make choices that promote health today so I will be ready to do God's work tomorrow. I believe that it is God's will for me to be healed. Let it be done in Jesus's name!

PURSUE DAILY

12

PURSUE COMMUNITY

"And let us consider how we may spur one another on toward love and good deeds, not giving up meeting together, as some are in the habit of doing, but encouraging one another—and all the more as you see the Day approaching."
Hebrews 10:24-25 NIV

THE EGG GAME

White Horse Ranch.

This was the place our church held youth camp every year, yet this was the first year I dared to go. My mom decided to help in the kitchen, so I had her nearby. Outside of my mother, all I saw were unfamiliar faces.

I grew up in a small town where I knew everyone, and everyone knew me. My friend group was practically solidified for me when I started preschool, so making new friends was something I wasn't good at. My family attended a church in the larger town over from us, and when I got old enough to start attending events with the youth group, I realized I didn't know anyone.

This feeling of not knowing people shook me to my core. I had great friendships at school and home but at church? No one. I nervously watched people walk in and out of the dining hall, trying to find someone who looked kind enough to be a friend. And suddenly, a girl plopped down next to me.

Her name was Anna. She started talking to me like we'd known each other all our lives. She was from Tupelo, Mississippi, in the state's northern part. I'm from Columbia, Mississippi, the southern part of the state, so we discussed differences in scenery, people, and schools. I'm unsure how she learned about our church camp or why she was at White Horse Ranch, but I'm glad she was there.

We bunked together that night, and having a friend gave me the confidence to participate in activities and even go up in front of everyone to participate in a group game. The next day, however, we played a *horrible* game. (If you're a youth pastor reading this, don't *ever* play this game with your youth!). I don't know the game title, but it started by standing and facing your partner. You would each lock arms and walk around as one unit. On each person's back was an egg that was duct taped to them. The object of the game was to use your teammate's back to crush as many eggs on other people's backs as possible. *Legendary*.

So, of course, I looked for Anna to be my partner. However, I couldn't find her, so I partnered up with another girl I didn't know. We locked arms and walked around the field, trying to move each other out of the way when people came to smash our eggs. But low and behold, as two tiny girls in a field of youth, a high school guy got close to us, and *SLAM*. There went my egg. And my peace. And my confidence.

I fell to the ground, embarrassed and physically hurt from the weight of a giant teenager forcing himself on my back. It took the breath out of me, and all I could do was cry. As any sophisticated pre-teen would, I got up and ran to my mom. Through the tears, I explained what happened, and after begging, we packed our bags and went home.

Later that night, I realized I'd never had a chance to say goodbye to Anna, and I was heartbroken. To this day, we've never spoken again (primarily because you don't share important details like your last name or phone number as kids). So, if you're an Anna from Tupelo and remember having a friend get smashed in an egg game at youth camp, hit me up.

My friendship with Anna was short, but it gave me the confidence I needed to get through the first days of camp. I felt insecure and weak when I was alone, but when I had a friend, I felt more empowered and free to be myself. Even though our time together at camp didn't end the way I'd like it to, I still remember the feeling of having a friend who cared about me. The feeling of having *community* that cared about me.

We mentioned community briefly in the last chapter, but in this section, we will further dive into the importance of community as believers and why it is necessary for a healthy Christian life. Like Anna provided companionship for me in a difficult time, I believe God has special people in your life to ensure you don't do this alone.

WHAT IS COMMUNITY?
"They devoted themselves to the apostles' teaching and to fellowship, to the breaking of bread and to prayer."
Acts 2:42 NIV

"Community" is defined as "a feeling of fellowship with others, as a result of sharing common attitudes, interests, and goals."[1] In other words, community happens when people connect. Our theme verse for this section, Acts 2:42, mentions the importance of fellowship to the believers in the New Testament. This verse shares that community was so important that they *devoted* themselves to it, along with learning about God.

The word "fellowship" in Acts 2:42 is interchangeable with "community." The original Greek definition is "joint participation."[2] You see, the thing about community is that it takes effort from more than one person. To truly be in community with others, there must be joint participation between two or more individuals. So, if you're shy and don't like big groups of people, don't worry! You can be in community if you're hanging out with one person. If you're a social butterfly and love big crowds, you're in for a treat! Community includes groups, large or small, that connect over a common purpose and put effort into their shared relationship.

The critical thing to remember about community is that healthy community thrives on common ground. It is essential to have people in your life who can give you an outside perspective, but it is also necessary to have people in your life with shared beliefs and interests. Without common ground, there is nothing to build a healthy relationship.

Your community can look like friends from school, family members, a church group, or your team at work. However, even though you may be in situations where you're surrounded by a particular community daily, they don't necessarily have to be *your* community. For example, you may go to school every day and not have a single friend in your class, but you have tons of best friends at church! While you may not always determine who you are around, you can choose who you let into your life.

WHY DO I NEED COMMUNITY?

"Resist him, standing firm in the faith, because you know that the family of believers throughout the world is undergoing the same kind of sufferings." - 1 Peter 5:9 NIV

The theme verse for this section is the same verse we used in Chapter 9 when we discussed awareness. Isn't it cool how all these topics connect?

1 Peter 5:9 encourages us, as believers, to resist the enemy and stand firm in our faith because we know that the "family of believers" worldwide is going through the same things we are experiencing. As much as it may pain you to hear this, *you are not the only one in your situation.* The thoughts of "it's only me" or "no one will ever understand" are lies from the enemy to keep you isolated and alone. Somewhere, someone is going through a situation very similar to yours. Somewhere, someone understands exactly how you feel. How do I know this? Because 1 Peter 5:9 says that a family of believers is experiencing the same struggles.[3]

Every time I read this verse, I think of a girl in my choir class in high school. One day, she was crying in class, and I checked on her. I simply said, "Hey, what's wrong?" And at that, she shot back at me and said, "My best friend's mom just died. But you wouldn't understand!" She got up and left, refusing to talk to me or even let me pray for her.

I understand that emotions and grief can make people act out of character. So, when she responded out of anger, I understood. But it was also sad because, as she walked away from me, I thought, "Wow. She has no idea that I actually understand *exactly* how she feels." She didn't know that my best friend passed away when I was nine, and a few years later, her mom passed away, too. She didn't know that I had experienced the same pain she was experiencing. She just assumed that no one could ever understand or comprehend how she felt, which kept her isolated in her pain.

We need to pursue community daily because it equips us to make it through the tough seasons in life. Through pursuing community, we find presence, purpose, and perspective in difficult situations that we would not be able to have if we went through things alone.

Presence

I don't know if you've ever found yourself in a situation where you needed someone to just sit with you, but I sure have. Sometimes, we face problems and don't need people to fix them. We need people to be *present* with us. This person, for me, is my husband. Austin is excellent at fixing things, but he understands that sometimes, all I need is for him to sit with me on the couch or hold me while we sleep. I need him to be present more than I need him to make everything perfect.

Community provides a physical presence when we are walking through difficult times. When we live in community with other believers, we see a physical representation of how we are surrounded in the spiritual realm. 2 Corinthians 5:7 reminds us that "we walk by faith, not by sight." Still, sometimes it's nice to see that you are surrounded and supported by people. Although we are never alone,[4] pursuing community provides physical proof that people (and the Lord) are present with us.

Purpose

Have you ever had those mornings where getting out of bed feels *impossible*? I had one of these mornings recently. Everything in me wanted to turn off my alarm, pull the covers over my face, and dive back into sleep, refusing the day's responsibilities. However, I knew I had to get out of bed, not because I *wanted* to but because I *needed* to. I had made commitments that day to others that I could not miss, and staying in bed was not a good reason to cancel on my community.

Community provides purpose in our lives. When we can't find a reason to live, work, or persevere for ourselves, we can almost always find a reason to push through for someone else. When we have community in our lives, we have a reason to be alive! We have a purpose. Our community holds us accountable for our commitments and our actions. They know our passions and giftings and push us towards our goals. Without community, we are left to ourselves to determine what is right and wrong for us, and while you may think that's freedom, it's actually restraint.

I want to take a moment to speak to those who have believed the lie that "you can do it on your own" or "it's just God and me, and that's how I like it." While our relationship with God is the most important one, God's Word makes it very clear that we are to continue living in community with people. Hebrews 10:25 tells us to "not give up meeting together, as some are in the habit of doing, but [to] encourage one another."

Right now, in 2023, many people are in the habit of not meeting together. Call it a post-pandemic world if you want, but this trend happened way before COVID-19 hit the earth. People have continued to be disconnected through social media and have isolated themselves behind false fronts. As Christians, however, we are called to break this trend. We are called to continue meeting together and encouraging each other. As we meet and encourage one another, it provides purpose for our lives!

Perspective

Our theme verse for this section, 1 Peter 5:9, says that we know the "family of believers throughout the world is undergoing the same kind of suffering" we are facing. While sometimes the last thing we want to hear is "I know exactly how you feel," it is often what we need to hear. This is because we need perspective.

Having a godly community provides you with perspective when going through difficult times. While the pain is real, we must understand that it cannot be all we see. Yes, taking care of ourselves and getting the help we need is important. However, past our pain, there are people who truly understand and need attention themselves.

Without community, we become isolated, and it's easy to become engulfed with self-pity. However, when we have people in our lives to bring perspective, we can take our eyes off ourselves and set them on those around us. When our perspective changes, we realize that we are not alone. Again, while the pain is real, perspective shows us that it is also temporary. Pain is temporary because, while there may be pain here on earth, there is no pain in heaven.[5] Getting around godly community reminds you to keep a heavenly perspective.

HOW DO I PURSUE COMMUNITY?
"A friend loves at all times, and a brother is born for a time of adversity."
Proverbs 17:17 NIV

By now, hopefully, you understand the importance of community and friendships. God created us for community. Regardless of your personality type, interests, activities, or desires, deep down, we all crave *connection*—a connection with God and people.

As we close out this chapter, let's discuss how we pursue community and find those friendships we crave.

Make choices that put yourself in community.

I am a homebody. I LOVE being home, and honestly, I love being home *alone*. I can do laundry, cook the meal I want, watch what I want on TV, and not worry about anyone else. It's wonderful. It's wonderful.

While there's nothing wrong with being an introvert or loving to be at home, there *is* something wrong with allowing those preferences to keep us from building community. If I never spent time with Austin because I enjoy being alone, how would our marriage be? If I never went out and did things with friends, how would my friendships be? If I never chose to put myself in community, how would my community be?

We all have our preferences. Some of us prefer alone time. Some of us prefer small groups. Some of us prefer large groups. Some of us like to be around people all the time because we can't stand alone time. However, building friendships comes when we engage in community despite our preferences.

We pursue community by making choices to put ourselves in community. I remember having a conversation with an old friend about dating. She was ready to start dating but hadn't had any success. Then, one morning, she shared with me a revelation. She realized that she hadn't had any success meeting a guy because she was never in a situation to meet a guy. Her routine was set—she went to work, the gym, and came home. She repeated this schedule every day. Yet, she never met anyone new in the same routine she had. So, to be in the position to meet someone, she had to go where she believed the kind of guy she would be interested in would be.

This is not just excellent dating advice. This is great community advice! If you want to find or make better friends, you've got to go where they are. Try out the different groups at your church. Identify a ministry where you'd like to volunteer. Pick a gym where you know some great people work out. Ask a mentor if you can spend a day with her. Pursue godly community by making choices that put you in community!

Be a friend first.

Proverbs 17:17 says that "a friend loves at all times." That sounds great on the receiving end. I mean, who wouldn't want to be loved at all times? Isn't that what we desire at our core—to be loved?

But what happens when you're on the *giving* end, not the *receiving* end? What happens when you're the one who needs to show love at all times, not *be* loved at all times? One of the biggest mistakes we can make is thinking that friendships just "happen." We meet a good group of people. They invite us to do everything. We hit it off immediately. And boom—we've built community.

However, that's not always how it works. Sometimes (I would say more times than not), community takes work. Friendship takes discipline. As unfortunate as it may be, there may not be people knocking down your door to be friends with you all the time. That's not meant to be harsh. It's intended to be realistic.

It's unrealistic and, honestly, selfish to think everyone else must work to build community except us. Sometimes, when we want friends, we have to be a friend first.

If you find yourself in a position where you're desperate for connection and community, try being a friend. Try loving at all times without receiving love first. Try inviting people to dinner or to participate in a fun activity together. You never know who is waiting for a friend just like you!

Know that you can't be everyone's friend, but you can be someone's friend.

After reading the last point, some of you are probably thinking, "Well, I've tried that! I've tried to be a friend, but they still don't like me!" And to that, I would ask: Why is it important for that particular person(s) to like you?

Here's something you must understand as you're building community: You can't be everyone's friend. It's not physically possible. As amazing as you are, you can only manage so many relationships. According to scientist Robin Dunbar, a person can only successfully manage 150 meaningful relationships.[6] While you may have more connections than that, thanks to social media or a social butterfly personality, it is still *impossible* to expect that you will be everyone's friend.

I'm not saying this to cast you down or make fun of you. I'm saying this to liberate you! So often, I see people trying to make friendships work that weren't meant to be. When I ask why it's so important that these people like them, the answers usually come down to popularity, status, and insecurity, and none of those are great reasons to pursue community with someone.

You can't be *everyone's* friend, but you can be *someone's* friend. It may not be working out with the people you thought you wanted to be friends with, but does that mean you don't have any options for friends? Of course not! Someone always needs a friend, and the friendships worth fighting for aren't those based on popularity, status, or insecurity. Friendships worth fighting for are based on love, grace, and encouragement. Consider asking yourself these questions when pursuing community:

- Does this person need a friend?
- Does this person make me better?
- Is this someone I can connect with?
- Is this someone I can grow with?

Pursue the friendships and community that encourage you, not discourage you. If you leave your time with someone questioning your self-worth or discouraged, she is probably not the right friend for you. Even if you thought that person would be your best friend ever, it's okay to let it go.

Often, we find friendships in the most unexpected places. One of my best friends, Hannah, is entirely different than me. We are opposites in every way, except we both love the Lord a lot. We were on our way to the beach once, and a song came on our playlist. I said, "Turn it up! I love this song!" as Hannah said, "Ew, turn this off! I hate this song!"

Even though Hannah and I have differences, we found common ground on what matters. We both needed a friend. We make each other better. We connect well and grow together. And I believe God has friends and community in store for you that will do the same. You just have to pursue them daily!

Daily Declaration

"I know I was not created to do life alone. Therefore, I choose to put myself where I can build godly community with others. I commit to investing in friendships with others. I'm not afraid to make the first move when it comes to building community. I will put myself out there and trust God to bring me the right friends at the right time. Even if people reject me, I know God will never reject me, and He has placed people in my life who love and believe in me!"

13

PURSUE THE END GOAL

"I want to know Christ—yes, to know the power of His resurrection and participation in His sufferings, becoming like Him in His death, and so, somehow, attaining to the resurrection from the dead. Not that I have already obtained all this, or have already arrived at my goal, but I press on to take hold of that for which Christ Jesus took hold of me. Brothers and sisters, I do not consider myself yet to have taken hold of it. But one thing I do: Forgetting what is behind and straining toward what is ahead, I press on toward the goal to win the prize for which God has called me heavenward in Christ Jesus."
Philippians 3:10-14 NIV

TWO HALVES MAKE A WHOLE

One of the most important days of my life was college decision day. I had my acceptance letters on the table, pro-and-con list in tow, and was ready to decide. It was April of my senior year of high school, and my window of choosing where I went to school next year was slowly but surely closing. I had three choices for school:

Mississippi College, the University of North Alabama, and Highlands College. I had spent countless hours researching and conducting campus visits to decide where I would go. The entire time, I knew I would end up at Highlands College, but one thing was holding me back: the half-marathon.

Highlands College holds a half-marathon each year for full-time ministry school students. Since I was looking into the full-time program, I knew that would be a reality for me. And I'll be honest. It terrified me.

I am not a runner. Despite comments about me having the "perfect runner's body" and my dad's history as a track and field coach, running never seemed to be my cup of tea. I hated it so much that it was the only factor keeping me from attending ministry school. Isn't that sad?

Looking at the acceptance letters on the table, I knew in my heart that Highlands College was the correct choice. I decided to attend in the fall, and the rest is history. When I began classes, I was surprised to hear that the half-marathon was being held in the spring. It gave me months to train, and I joined a running group. I wasn't the quickest runner and didn't run the 13.1 miles entirely, but I finished. I didn't do my best in the first round, but I knew that the following year, I'd have another chance.

However, I didn't realize that the following year, the half-marathon was moved to the fall, which meant that I'd be running 13.1 miles again *in just a few months*. I was looking forward to training the entire year! I was going to start eating better and pushing myself more. But in just a few months, I'd be running the same race again.

I saw the timeline narrowing, so I started training. I showed up at 6 a.m. for runs in freezing weather when no one else did. I pushed myself and trained as hard as I could. And when the second half-marathon rolled around, my main goal was to finish in under three hours.

If you know anything about races, finishing a half in under three hours is very doable. However, for a non-runner like me, it was a big goal to reach. Finishing in under three hours would mean I'd cut off more than 40 minutes of my time from the spring (yeah, we won't talk about that...). When race day came, I ran my race, even though it was sooner than I thought it would be. And sure enough, I crossed the finish line minutes before the 3-hour mark.

Am I telling you this story to celebrate my fantastic finish time and athletic abilities? *Obviously* not. A five-year-old could finish a half-marathon in less than three hours. Instead, I am telling you this story to make some necessary points for our discussion on pursuing the end goal.

First, to reach my goal, I had to have a goal. I would have had nothing to aim for if I didn't have a goal (like the first time I ran the half-marathon). Without something to aim for, there was no reason to run.

Second, the time to achieve my goal came quicker than I thought. While I was expecting a year of recovery and training, I only had six months to train. While this is a straightforward, practical example, some of you have been met with timelines you didn't think you would. You've been given a certain amount of time to spend with someone you love. Your time at your school is ending. You're moving months before you thought you would. A relationship you thought would last forever only lasted a few weeks.

You see, the thing about goals is that they can change—because circumstances can change. As much as I want to achieve my goals, and *I do want to achieve them*, I can only control what I can control. It wasn't my responsibility to set a date for the half-marathon. It was my responsibility to train for what was coming.

We can't always control our circumstances, but we can control what we do in them.

While we can have many goals that change over our lives, one goal does not change: the end goal. This end goal is hard to prepare for because we don't know when it will happen. It's challenging to prepare for because it's the most unnatural thing for us to pursue. But this end goal is the most impactful thing to prepare for because it's what will last *forever*.

WHAT IS THE END GOAL?
"But seek first His kingdom and His righteousness, and all these things will be given to you as well".
Matthew 6:33 NIV

The end goal, simply put, is eternity. Heaven. God's Kingdom. All the topics we've discussed this far in *Pursue Daily* have been to get us to this conversation. Philippians 3:20 says, "We are citizens of heaven, where the Lord Jesus Christ lives. And we are eagerly waiting for him to return as our Savior." Regardless of how we meet Jesus, whether through going to heaven or Jesus returning to earth, our end goal is to see Jesus and spend eternity with Him.

Pursuing the end goal of eternity has everything to do with what we do here on earth. If God wanted us in heaven immediately after we got saved, He would have made that part of His plan. That's not the plan, though. The plan is for us to be saved and live on earth so that we can share the love of God with everyone we can. Whether or not people realize it, eternity is *everyone's* "end goal," and it's either heaven or hell.

I believe God desires for you to understand how important this is. Eternity is our end goal! Matthew 6:33 says we must "seek first His Kingdom and His righteousness." This means that while we're living, we can pursue eternity by constantly pursuing God's will on earth, as it is in heaven.

WHY DO I NEED TO PURSUE THE END GOAL?

"But seek first His kingdom and His righteousness, and all these things will be given to you as well."
Matthew 6:33 NIV

We pursue the end goal because it's our purpose. In God's Kingdom, everything hangs on the balance of eternity. Although we're pursuing eternity, we can get glimpses of heaven right where we are on earth. John 10:10 says that Jesus came to give us "life" so we could "have [life] to the full." Not only did Jesus come to give us abundant eternal life, but He also came to provide us with abundant life *right now*. By pursuing the end goal, we can experience heaven on earth!

As mentioned above, Matthew 6:33 says that "all these things" will be available as we seek the end goal. So, what do "all these things" entail? Let's look at the list from earlier in Matthew 6:

- Eating and drinking
- Your body
- Clothing[1]

Matthew 6:24-25 teaches about not worrying, specifically about the simple provisions people need. Jesus says in Matthew 6:32 that God "knows that we need" these things. He created us to run on food and water. He understands that we need healthy bodies to experience the fullness of life. He knows we need clothing to cover our bodies (although His OG plan in the Garden of Eden was different).[2] This section of Scripture is not saying that these things are unimportant; on the contrary, this Scripture confirms that these things are essential. However, these things are not as important as pursuing God and His Kingdom.

We must pursue the end goal daily because it is the prerequisite for every other thing we need. In other words, if we have heaven on our minds, we have satisfaction in our hearts.

If our primary focus every day is pursuing the Kingdom of God, then we don't have time to focus on what could easily distract us from what matters most. Even Jesus said that we should not "worry about tomorrow, for tomorrow will worry about itself."[3] There will always be things vying for our attention. However, when we pursue the end goal, we are reminded of the peace, presence, and eminence of God and His Kingdom and the future that awaits us.

HOW DO I PURSUE THE END GOAL?

"If God gives such attention to the appearance of wildflowers—most of which are never even seen—don't you think He'll attend to you, take pride in you, do His best for you? What I'm trying to do here is to get you to relax, to not be so preoccupied with getting, so you can respond to God's giving. People who don't know God and the way He works fuss over these things, but you know both God and how He works. Steep your life in God-reality, God-initiative, God-provisions. Don't worry about missing out. You'll find all your everyday human concerns will be met."
Matthew 6:30-33 MSG

As we conclude this chapter on pursuing the end goal and our journey of pursuing daily together, let's talk about what it looks like to actively put everything we've learned into practice and pursue the end goal of eternity.

I believe Eugene Peterson said it best in *The Message* paraphrase of the Bible. I stumbled across this version of Matthew 6 recently, and when I saw these three items listed, I knew it was important. Seeking God's Kingdom and righteousness first looks like pursuing God's reality, initiatives, and provisions.

I knew these items would find their way onto my daily prayer list the moment I read them. Nearly every morning, I try to pray through these three areas, actively seeking God's Kingdom first. Praying through God's reality, initiatives, and provisions is a great way to pursue the end goal, and I would like to introduce this outline to you as a guide to pursuing the end goal daily.

Focus on God's Reality.

We know from Ephesians 6:12 that there is such a thing as the "heavenly realms." In other words, there is a spiritual reality beyond what we can see, and this reality is God's reality.

Pursuing the end goal daily means focusing on God's reality. When we "set [our] minds on things above,"[4] we pursue God's reality. We may not necessarily see everything in the spiritual realm with our eyes, but we can mentally have the mind of Christ that is focused on God's reality.

God's reality looks like victory, health, peace, joy, love, patience, and humility (and I'm sure the list could go on and on!). As you pursue God's reality daily, think about it with these questions:

- What is God doing right now?
- What is God seeing right now?
- What is God feeling right now?

The only way to get these answers is through prayerfully reading God's Word. As you process these questions, you have a visual representation of God's reality. *Where is God?* He's on the throne, but His Spirit lives in our hearts. *What is God doing?* He's watching us, guiding us, leading us, protecting us, and loving us.

What is God seeing? There are many hurting people on earth but many rejoicing people in heaven. *What is God feeling?* Love for every person and pain for those who don't know Him yet.

This is God's reality, and as we seek the end goal daily, His reality becomes our reality.

Focus on God's Initiatives.

An "initiative" is "an act of strategy intended to resolve a difficulty or improve a situation."[5] There are initiatives God has set in motion, which are things God cares for deeply. There are global initiatives that God put in place to resolve problems and improve situations, both temporary and eternal. There are also personal initiatives He's started in your life—specifically for *you*. When we focus on God's initiatives and the strategies He's put in place, He will take care of our needs. As you take some time to pray through and focus on God's initiatives, you are pursuing the end goal. Consider some of the following as you pray through God's initiatives:

- **Salvation** - It is God's will for every person to be saved.[6] Salvation was God's idea, and He wants to see every person come to know Him through choice, not force.
- **Marriage** - God created marriage. Marriage is the institution God designed to represent His relationship with His Church.[7] The sanctity of marriage, between one man and one woman, and reproduction were His initiatives.[8] Therefore, we should pray for the protection and success of marriages as God designed them.
- **Healing** - God created us. He did not create sickness, illness, or pain, but He does use healing to provide relief and wholeness to our bodies, souls, and spirits. Healing was God's initiative, and He desires for us to be healed.[9]

- **The Local Church** - God created the Church. As we see in John 16, God never intended for Jesus Himself to be on earth forever.[10] Instead, God intended for apostles, prophets, evangelists, shepherds, and teachers to "equip the saints for the work of ministry, for building up the body of Christ."[11] The "body of Christ" is His Church, and the Church is built and equipped by people He has called. Local churches are a part of the big "C" Church that encompasses all believers, and we must pray for protection and growth for every church and leader that preaches the Gospel of Jesus.
- **Serving** - As seen throughout the life of Jesus, God's initiative is to serve. One could almost label this as God's initiative to *love*. Love and serving go hand-in-hand. You cannot do one without the other. Matthew 10:45 says, "The Son of Man did not come to be served, but to serve, and to give His life as a ransom for many." Jesus displayed the initiative of serving others instead of expecting to be served. Therefore, we should pray and ask God to give us opportunities to love and serve others.

As you continue to read God's Word and grow in your faith, you will see other initiatives God put into play. In addition to His global initiatives for humanity, as we mentioned earlier, God also has initiatives He's planned for you! Don't know what they are? Think through these questions and see if you can identify an initiative that God has begun in your life:

- What am I passionate about?
- What opportunities are in front of me right now?
- What makes me feel alive?
- What (or who) do I feel drawn to?

- What are my biggest dreams?
- What gifts or skills has God equipped me with?

Is there an area, career path, hobby, etc., that combines all the above? If so, it may be God beginning something new in your life! Consider pursuing this initiative as a way to pursue the end goal.

Focus on God's Provisions.

What a shame to be so caught up in what we want that we forget what God has already supplied. This part truly encompasses Matthew 6:30-33, which encourages us "to not be so preoccupied with getting, so we can respond to God's giving."

When we focus on God's provisions, we are making time to 1) thank God for what He's done and 2) depend on Him for what needs to be done. As we pursue the end goal by focusing on God's provisions, we realize that most of the things we tend to worry about are entirely outside our control. We stress ourselves out trying to provide for ourselves in some areas when God never asked us to provide. He asked us to *receive*.

As we focus on God's provisions—life, joy, peace, health, breath, relationships—we realize how big our God is and how small we are. We cannot meet our own needs because we were never created to be our own God. Therefore, we focus on God's provisions, giving thanks for what He's done and anticipating what He will do.

C.S. Lewis once said, "Aim at heaven, and you will get earth 'thrown in;' aim at earth, and you will get neither."[12] As we pursue the end goal of heaven, we are aiming for the highest goal possible. Nothing on this earth will *ever* compare to heaven. No amount of money. No amount of followers. No amount of influence. Heaven is the end goal. And, when we aim for heaven, not only do we get eternal life, but we also get an abundant life thrown in here on earth. And here's the cool part: Other people will see the abundant life we're living and want to be part of it. Pursuing the end goal isn't only about you; it's about introducing eternal life to those around you.

Eternal life is the greatest gift that anyone can receive from the Lord, but God also wants to give us the gift of abundant life here on earth. When we pursue the end goal of heaven, we will get everything we've ever wanted and more. A mind set on heaven can never be disappointed. Why? Because there is *hope* in heaven.

If you want to live a life that matters, aim for heaven.

Daily Declaration

"I believe heaven is my home. I also believe that I have a purpose to accomplish here on earth. Therefore, I will pursue the end goal of heaven daily by focusing on God's reality, initiatives, and provision. I commit to living an abundant life and sharing the Gospel with as many people as I can so I can bring as many people with me as possible to heaven. Thank you, Lord, for eternal life and abundant life!"

PURSUE DAILY

CONCLUSION
CONTINUE TO PURSUE DAILY

Wow. What a journey this has been.

As we wrap up our time together, I want to thank you for coming on this journey with me. The process of sanctification, growing into who God wants us to be, can be a daunting and overwhelming task. Still, it is the most beautiful, fulfilling, and life-giving process any Christian could experience.

I hope you have learned more about God, the Bible, and yourself over the last thirteen chapters. I pray that you achieved whatever goal you set out to accomplish when you began this book. Ultimately, I pray that this book made life simpler instead of more complex.

The whole idea of *Pursue Daily* is to make sanctification simple. Now, I know some people who would argue with me about the importance of simplicity in Christianity. And while we could get nose-deep in theology, apologetics, and all that jazz, I truly believe God simply wants us to experience Him daily. He wants our daily encounters with Him to make us more and more like Jesus.

Throughout this book, we've discussed thirteen pursuits outlined for Christians in the Bible:

- Pursue God
- Pursue Faith
- Pursue Righteousness
- Pursue Love
- Pursue Peace
- Pursue Humility
- Pursue Forgiveness
- Pursue Awareness
- Pursue Your Gifting
- Pursue Health
- Pursue Community
- Pursue the End Goal

Are there more than these thirteen? Absolutely! God's Word is chock-full of pursuits, journeys, challenges, and adventures that God invites us to join, and I hope that your time with these thirteen topics has sparked a desire to learn more about God and His Word through other pursuits.

In closing, I want to remind you of something significant. I don't know what the following months or years will hold for you. I don't know if you'll return to this book or if it was a simple one-and-done. However, I want to encourage you that the journey to pursue God daily never ends. As we said in the beginning, there is no "arriving" with God. While we're still breathing, the journey is still worth traveling.

There is always more of God to discover, so never stop pursuing Him. Pursue daily and watch how your life is transformed.

DISCUSSION QUESTIONS

Chapter 1 – Pursue God
1. What has God taught me throughout this chapter about pursuing God?
2. What is the one area (worship, prayer, and Bible reading) I need to work on the most? How can I get better at it?
3. What is one thing I learned while reading this chapter that I can share with someone this week?
4. What is God saying to me right now?

Chapter 2 – Pursue Faith
1. What situations, good or bad, have occurred in the last year that have affected my faith? How have they affected it?
2. Through reading this chapter, has my faith become sharper, or has it become duller? Why?
3. Knowing what I know now about faith, what situations in my life could God be using to strengthen my faith?
4. What is God saying to me right now about my personal journey to pursuing faith daily?

Chapter 3 – Pursue Righteousness
1. Have I made choices that resulted in righteousness, or have I made choices that resulted in recklessness?
2. What does God's Word say about me?
3. What does God's Word say is "good"?
4. Write down a few things that the world says are "good." Write down what God's Word says about these things. Do they agree or disagree?

Chapter 4 – Pursue Love
1. Out of the different kinds of love (family, friends, romantic, and Godly), which one am I the best at? Which one am I the worst at? Why?
2. What is my favorite Bible verse about love? Why?
3. How can I practically love the people in my life this week?
4. Who is someone I have loved well? Who is someone that I haven't loved well? What is God saying to me about these people right now?

Chapter 5 – Pursue Peace
1. What are the top three things in life I tend to worry about? Why?
2. What are some Bible verses I could use to pray over the situations that make me anxious?
3. Who has God placed in my life to pray and petition with me?
4. What am I thankful for?

Chapter 6 – Pursue Purity
1. Have I seen purity as a status or lifestyle in the past? Why?
2. Is there anything that's been polluting my body, soul, or spirit? What is it, and where is it coming from?

3. What is my view of the Bible?
4. How can I pursue the path of purity this week?

Chapter 7 – Pursue Humility
1. Do I believe I've been living a humble life this far? Why or why not?
2. How has my view of "submission" affected my relationship with God and others?
3. Which area—Christ, covering, or community—do I need to work on submitting to the most?
4. What is a practical way that I can live a life of submission this week?

Chapter 8 – Pursue Forgiveness
1. What did I think of when I heard the word "forgiveness" before reading this chapter?
2. What has changed about the way I see forgiveness?
3. Who do I need to forgive?
4. How can I forgive them?

Chapter 9 – Pursue Awareness
1. What did God show me in this chapter? Did He make me aware of anything?
2. What practical steps can I take to become more aware of the enemy's schemes?
3. What practical steps can I take to become more aware of God's Word?
4. How can I help my friends become more aware?

Chapter 10 – Pursue Your Gifting
1. What are my spiritual gifts?
2. How am I using my spiritual gifts?

3. Are there gifts that I don't have that I want? Why?
4. What ways can I use my spiritual gifts this week?

Chapter 11 – Pursue Health
1. What area(s)—physical, emotional, spiritual, social, mental—am I healthy? What area(s) do I need help?
2. For the areas in which I need help, what has kept me from seeking healing in the past?
3. What do I need healing from?
4. What are the practical steps I can take to seek healing in these areas?

Chapter 12 – Pursue Community
1. What kind of community do I have in my life right now?
2. What kind of community do I want in my life right now?
3. What choices can I make to put myself in community?
4. Who can I be a friend to today?

Chapter 13 – Pursue the End Goal
1. What are some goals I want to accomplish in my lifetime?
2. What would it look like to practically pursue heaven today?
3. What are some God-initiatives (things that God has ordained) that I can see in my life?
4. What ways has God provided for me in the past? What am I trusting Him to provide for in the future?

NOTES

Introduction
1. "Sanctification," Oxford Languages, 2023, https://languages.oup.com/google-dictionary-en/.
2. Gregg R. Allison, *50 Core Truths of the Christian Faith: A Guide to Understanding and Teaching Theology* (Grand Rapids: Baker Publishing Group, 2018), 265.

Chapter 1 – Pursue God
1. "Engizō," Blue Letter Bible, 2023, https://www.blueletterbible.org/lexicon/g1448/niv/mgnt/0-1/.
2. See Joshua 1:9.
3. Matthew 26:31 (NIV).
4. See 1 Thessalonians 5:23.
5. See Genesis 1:27.
6. See 2 Corinthians 13:14 and Matthew 28:19.
7. Hitte, 2023.
8. See 1 John 4:19.
9. 1 John 4:19 (NIV).
10. See Ephesians 2:8.

11. Donald S. Whitney, *Spiritual Disciplines for the Christian Life* (Colorado Springs: Tyndale House Publishers, Inc., 2014).
12. Mark L. Knapp & John A. Daly, *The SAGE Handbook of Interpersonal Communication* (London: SAGE Publications, Inc., 2011), 239.
13. See Genesis 3.
14. See Genesis 17.
15. See Exodus 33.
16. See Psalm 59.
17. See Daniel 6.
18. See Luke 22.
19. See Psalm 119:105.
20. See 2 Timothy 3:16.
21. See Hebrews 13:8.

Chapter 2 – Pursue Faith

1. "Faith," Oxford Languages, 2023, https://languages.oup.com/google-dictionary-en/.
2. "Pistis," Blue Letter Bible, 2023, https://www.blueletterbible.org/lexicon/g4102/niv/mgnt/0-1/.
3. "Pistis," Blue Letter Bible, 2023, https://www.blueletterbible.org/lexicon/g4102/niv/mgnt/0-1/.
4. See Exodus 3:14.
5. See Deuteronomy 31:6.
6. See John 3:16.
7. See John 16:33.
8. See 1 Corinthians 12:9.
9. See Psalm 119:68.
10. See 1 John 1:5.
11. James 1:2-3 (NIV).

12. See James 1:4.

Chapter 3 – Pursue Righteousness
1. "Dikaiosynē," Blue Letter Bible, 2023, https://www.blueletterbible.org/lexicon/g1343/niv/mgnt/0-1/.
2. "Dikaiosynē," Blue Letter Bible, 2023, https://www.blueletterbible.org/lexicon/g1343/niv/mgnt/0-1/.
3. "Dikaiosynē," Blue Letter Bible, 2023, https://www.blueletterbible.org/lexicon/g1343/niv/mgnt/0-1/.
4. "Righteousness," Oxford Languages, 2023, https://languages.oup.com/google-dictionary-en/.
5. See Genesis 1:27.
6. See Matthew 5:20.
7. See Romans 3:22 and 1 Corinthians 1:30.
8. See Matthew 6:5.
9. See Matthew 12:34.
10. See Philippians 4:8.
11. See Romans 12:2.

Chapter 4 – Pursue Love
1. "Agapē," Blue Letter Bible, 2023, https://www.blueletterbible.org/lexicon/g26/niv/mgnt/0-1/.
2. Hitte, 2022.
3. 1 Corinthians 13:1-3 (NIV).
4. Matthew 22:39 (NIV).
5. "Agapaō," Blue Letter Bible, 2023, https://www.blueletterbible.org/lexicon/g25/niv/mgnt/0-1/.

6. "Agapaō," Blue Letter Bible, 2023, https://www.blueletterbible.org/lexicon/g25/niv/mgnt/0-1/.
7. "Proslambanō," Blue Letter Bible, 2023, https://www.blueletterbible.org/lexicon/g4355/niv/mgnt/0-1/.
8. See Romans 12:15.
9. See Romans 12:15.
10. Galatians 6:2 (NLT).
11. See Matthew 11:28.

Chapter 5 – Pursue Peace
1. "Eirēnē," Blue Letter Bible, 2023, https://www.blueletterbible.org/lexicon/g1515/esv/mgnt/0-1/.
2. "Eirēnē," Blue Letter Bible, 2023, https://www.blueletterbible.org/lexicon/g1515/esv/mgnt/0-1/.
3. "Eirēnē," Blue Letter Bible, 2023, https://www.blueletterbible.org/lexicon/g1515/esv/mgnt/0-1/.
4. See Isaiah 9:6.
5. "Poreuō," Blue Letter Bible, 2023, https://www.blueletterbible.org/lexicon/g4198/niv/mgnt/0-1/.
6. "Proseuchē," Blue Letter Bible, 2023, https://www.blueletterbible.org/lexicon/g4335/niv/mgnt/0-1/.
7. Philippians 4:6 (NIV).
8. "Deēsis," Blue Letter Bible, 2023, https://www.blueletterbible.org/lexicon/g1162/niv/mgnt/0-1/.

9. Philippians 4:6 (NIV).
10. See John 16:33.
11. Philippians 4:7 (NIV).

Chapter 6 – Pursue Purity
1. "Katharos," Blue Letter Bible, 2023, https://www.blueletterbible.org/lexicon/g2513/niv/mgnt/0-1/.
2. "Purity," Oxford Languages, 2023, https://languages.oup.com/google-dictionary-en/.
3. "Adulteration," Oxford Languages, 2023, https://languages.oup.com/google-dictionary-en/.
4. See Psalm 139:14.
5. "Contamination," Oxford Languages, 2023, https://languages.oup.com/google-dictionary-en/.
6. "Horaō," Blue Letter Bible, 2023, https://www.blueletterbible.org/lexicon/g3708/niv/mgnt/0-1/.
7. See Isaiah 1:18, 1 John 1:7, 1 John 1:9, Hebrews 9:14, Hebrews 9:22, John 14:6, Ephesians 2:13-14, Ephesians 2:18, and Ephesians 3:12.
8. Mike Sullivan, "Five Views on Sanctification," Dwell Community Church, 2023. https://dwellcc.org/learning/essays/five-views-sanctification.
9. See John 1:29 and 1 Corinthians 15:3.
10. Isaiah 1:18 (NIV).
11. Hebrews 9:28 (NIV).
12. See Hebrews 9:11-28.
13. Revelation 21:5 (NIV).

14. "Šāmar," Blue Letter Bible, 2023, https://www.blueletterbible.org/lexicon/h8104/niv/wlc/0-1/.
15. "Over Half of Gen Z Teens Feel Motivated to Learn More About Jesus," Barna Group, Inc., February 1, 2023, https://www.barna.com/research/teens-and-jesus/.
16. "Over Half of Gen Z Teens Feel Motivated to Learn More About Jesus," Barna Group, Inc., February 1, 2023, https://www.barna.com/research/teens-and-jesus/.
17. See Hebrews 13:8.

Chapter 7 – Pursue Humility
1. See Isaiah 60:1.
2. Matthew 5:5 (NIV).
3. "Tapeinophyrosynē," Blue Letter Bible, 2023, https://www.blueletterbible.org/lexicon/g5012/niv/mgnt/0-1/.
4. "Tapeinophyrosynē," Blue Letter Bible, 2023, https://www.blueletterbible.org/lexicon/g5012/niv/mgnt/0-1/.
5. See Mark 6:30-31.
6. See Mark 6:3.
7. Rick Warren, *The Purpose Driven Life: What on Earth am I Here for?* (Grand Rapids: Zondervan, 2012), 149.
8. Ruth 4:14 (NIV).
9. Robert D. Jones, *Pursuing Peace: A Christian Guide to Handling Our Conflicts* (Wheaton: Crossway, 2012), 113.
10. "Yir'â," Blue Letter Bible, 2023, https://www.blueletterbible.org/lexicon/h3374/niv/wlc/0-1/.

11. "Hypotassō," Blue Letter Bible, 2023, https://www.blueletterbible.org/lexicon/g5293/niv/mgnt/0-1/.
12. See Ephesians 5:24-25.
13. See Ephesians 5:24-25.
14. See Proverbs 3:34 and James 4:6.
15. Romans 13:1 (NIV).
16. See Philippians 2:6-8.

Chapter 8 – Pursue Forgiveness
1. "Aphiēmi," Blue Letter Bible, 2023, https://www.blueletterbible.org/lexicon/g863/niv/mgnt/0-1/.
2. "Forgive," Oxford Languages, 2023, https://languages.oup.com/google-dictionary-en/.
3. Yasmin Anwar, "How Many Different Human Emotions Are There?" The Greater Good Science Center at the University of California, Berkley, 2017, https://greatergood.berkeley.edu/article/item/how_many_different_human_emotions_are_there.
4. The Beatles, "Let it Be," recorded January 1969, track 1 on *Let It Be,* Apple, EMI, and Olympic Sound, compact disc.
5. See Romans 12:19.
6. See Ephesians 4:32.
7. Galatians 2:20 (NIV).
8. Ephesians 2:1 (NIV).
9. See Matthew 12:31.
10. John 8:32 (NIV).
11. Matthew 5:44 (NIV).
12. See John 3:16.
13. Luke 23:34 (NIV).
14. See Psalm 136.

Chapter 9 – Pursue Awareness
1. See Genesis 50:20.
2. "Agnoeō," Blue Letter Bible, 2023, https://www.blueletterbible.org/lexicon/g50/niv/mgnt/0-1/.
3. Romans 8:11 (NIV).
4. Isaiah 1:18 (NIV).
5. See Luke 10:18.
6. See Isaiah 14:12-15.
7. 2 Chronicles 20:15 (NIV).
8. "Anthistēmi," Blue Letter Bible, 2023, https://www.blueletterbible.org/lexicon/g436/niv/mgnt/0-1/.
9. "Pistis," Blue Letter Bible, 2023, https://www.blueletterbible.org/lexicon/g4102/niv/mgnt/0-1/.

Chapter 10 – Pursue Your Gifting
1. "Charisma," Blue Letter Bible, 2023, https://www.blueletterbible.org/lexicon/g5486/niv/mgnt/0-1/.
2. "Charisma," Blue Letter Bible, 2023, https://www.blueletterbible.org/lexicon/g5486/niv/mgnt/0-1/.
3. See Ephesians 2:10.
4. See Romans 12:6.
5. See Romans 12:2.
6. See Matthew 25:14-28.
7. Matthew 25:23 (NIV).
8. "Zēloō," Blue Letter Bible, 2023, https://www.blueletterbible.org/lexicon/g2206/kjv/tr/0-1/.

Chapter 11 – Pursue Health

1. See Isaiah 53:5.
2. See 3 John 1:1.
3. 3 John 1:2 (NASB).
4. "Hygiainō," Blue Letter Bible, 2023, https://www.blueletterbible.org/lexicon/g5198/kjv/tr/0-1/.
5. 3 John 1:2 (NASB).
6. Psalm 103:2 (NIV).
7. See Psalm 103:1-5.
8. "Psychē," Blue Letter Bible, 2023, https://www.blueletterbible.org/lexicon/g5590/kjv/tr/0-1/.
9. "Sōphronismos," Blue Letter Bible, 2023, https://www.blueletterbible.org/lexicon/g4995/kjv/tr/0-1/.
10. See Romans 8:6.
11. See 1 Corinthians 6:20.
12. See 1 Corinthians 6:19-20.
13. Ephesians 1:7 (NIV).
14. "Exomologeō," Blue Letter Bible, 2023, https://www.blueletterbible.org/lexicon/g1843/kjv/tr/0-1/.
15. "Paraptōma," Blue Letter Bible, 2023, https://www.blueletterbible.org/lexicon/g3900/kjv/tr/0-1/.
16. James 5:16 (NIV).
17. James 5:16 (NIV).
18. Revelation 12:11 (KJV).

Chapter 12 – Pursue Community

1. "Community," Oxford Languages, 2023, https://languages.oup.com/google-dictionary-en/.
2. "Koinōnia," Blue Letter Bible, 2023, https://www.blueletterbible.org/lexicon/g2842/niv/mgnt/0-1/.
3. See 1 Peter 5:9.
4. See Joshua 1:9.
5. See Revelation 21:4.
6. Patrik Lindenfors et al. "'Dunbar's Number' Deconstructed," *Biology Letters* 17, no. 5 (2021): 1-4, doi: 10.1098/rsbl.2021.0158

Chapter 13 – Pursue the End Goal

1. See Matthew 6:25-26.
2. See Genesis 3.
3. Matthew 6:34 (NIV).
4. Colossians 3:2 (NIV).
5. "Initiative," Oxford Languages, 2023, https://languages.oup.com/google-dictionary-en/.
6. See 1 Timothy 2:4.
7. See Ephesians 5:21-33.
8. See Genesis 1:28 and Genesis 2:24.
9. See Jeremiah 30:17 and Luke 6:19.
10. See John 16:7.
11. Ephesians 4:11-12 (NIV).
12. C.S. Lewis, *The Joyful Christian* (New York: Macmillan Publishing Company, 1977).

ABOUT THE AUTHOR

Emily Green is a Christian author passionate about equipping and encouraging people through God's Word. Emily grew up in south Mississippi and moved to Birmingham, Alabama, in 2012, where she graduated from high school and attended Highlands College. Emily graduated from Highlands College with a Certificate of Ministry Leadership in 2018, her Associate degree in Christian Ministry in 2018 from Southeastern University, and her Bachelor's degree in Ministerial Leadership in 2020 from Southeastern University. She received her Master's degree in Communication in May 2023 from Liberty University. Emily entered full-time ministry in 2018 and continues to serve in the local church. She currently works as a social media manager and copywriter.

Emily and her husband, Austin, serve on the pastoral team at Discover Life Church. They currently reside in Melbourne, Florida, and enjoy golfing, watching football, taking walks around their neighborhood, and hanging out with friends.